SELF-PUBLISHING BOOKS 101

A STEP-BY-STEP GUIDE TO PUBLISHING YOUR BOOK IN MULTIPLE FORMATS

Shelley Hitz and Heather Hart

Body and Soul Publishing
Colorado Springs, CO

Shelley Hitz
P.O. Box 6542
Colorado Springs, CO 80934
www.trainingauthors.com

Earnings Disclaimer: There is no promise or representation that you will make a certain amount of sales, or any sales, as a result of using the techniques that are outlined within this book. Any earnings, revenue, or results using these marketing strategies are strictly estimates and there is no guarantee that you will have the same results. You accept the risk that the earnings and income statements differ by individual. The use of our information, products and services should be based on your own due diligence and you agree that we are not liable for your success or failure.

Full Disclosure: Some of the links in this book may be affiliate links (excluding any and all links to Amazon) and we may earn a small commission when you make a purchase through them. By law (FTC), we must disclose this. However, we want to ensure you that we only endorse products and services we believe in and would or do use ourselves.

Book Layout ©2013 Book Design Templates
www.trainingauthors.com/booktemplates

Ordering Information:
Quantity sales. Special discounts are available on quantity purchases by corporations, associations, and others. For details, contact the "Special Sales Department" at the address above.

Self-Publishing Books 101 / Shelley Hitz and Heather Hart. – 2nd ed.

ISBN-13: 978-0692213353
ISBN-10: 069221335X

TABLE OF CONTENTS

If You Can Dream It, You Can Do It!

Self-publishing has never been easier! Now, with the recent advancements in technology, <u>anyone</u> can get published. It is not only simple, quick, and doable to get your ideas self-published, but will also save you money. It simply amazes me!

Honestly, *if you can dream it, you can do it!*

Hi, I'm Shelley Hitz, and not that long ago, I was in your shoes.

You see, in 2008, I was researching self-publishing options on the internet. I actually stumbled upon the idea when a friend of ours showed us his self-published book—boy was I impressed! His paperback book looked and felt great in my hands, <u>very</u> professional.

Then, I found out what he paid to self-publish it—practically nothing! Plus, he could order copies at his cost for just $2-3 per book. My jaw dropped!

1

"*I could do this,*" I thought to myself. I had to find out more.

And I did. A lot more.

In fact, I have self-published over 30 books in the last several years, have been able to quit my job as a Physical Therapist to write full-time, and have partnered with Heather Hart to help other authors successfully publish and market their books.

Not only that, but we have learned how to publish books as:

- Paperback books
- eBooks (on various platforms)
- AudioBooks
- And even translate them into other languages

And we would like to help you do the same.

We will take you <u>step-by-step</u> through the self-publishing process in this book.

How to Self-Publish a Book

There are many options for self-publishing. Believe me, I know. When I started researching self-publishing options, I had no idea what I was even looking for in a publisher. I had no idea what features to look for, or what questions to ask—I simply started my search.

Do You Know Where to Start in Your Self-Publishing Journey?

Whether you are just getting started or already have experience in self-publishing, we are here to be your virtual "coaches" helping you from the start to the finish—writing, formatting, book cover design, choosing a publisher, publishing in various formats, and finally marketing your book.

Does it sound overwhelming to learn how to publish a book? It doesn't have to be! Remember, a journey of one thousand steps begins with one. Whether you are a high powered executive publishing books for your company or a stay at home mom publishing books for your family, you can do this!

Eight Simple Steps to Get You Started Self-Publishing Books:

1) Choose a topic for your book, preferably one you are passionate about.
2) Write your book in a word processor (e.g., Microsoft Word)
3) Get your manuscript edited.
4) Choose a self-publishing platform.
5) Format your book into the file(s) and format(s) required by your chosen publishing platform or pay someone to do it for you.
6) Design your book cover or pay someone to do it for you.
7) Upload your files and approve the proof copies, if applicable with your self-publishing company.
8) Start actively marketing your book sales page and selling copies online and/or at events.

If you have already written your book, you can literally have it published and start selling copies online within a week. It really is that amazing! However, you want to make sure you publish a professional book. Therefore, we recommend that you do not skimp on the editing, interior design, and book cover design.

As you are getting started, it is important to realize there is no guaranteed success for a published author. Writing, publishing, and marketing books is hard work. And now, there is a lot more competition; therefore, you need to make sure you produce quality work to help your book stand out.

Hopefully, from our experience and research, you will save a few hours along the way—maybe even hundreds of hours! Your time is precious, right?

So What Are You Waiting For?

Let's get started!

WAIT!

*Before you dig in to the information in this book,
how would you like to score a $27 author training course - FREE?*

*Do you need help coming up with a
book marketing plan that works for you?*

*We want to give you our master book marketing plan template with
a PDF training report free of charge.*

Why?

Simply because we enjoy helping authors succeed.

*Claim your free copy at the link below:
www.trainingauthors.com/newsletter*

About Self-Publishing

D o you want to learn more about self-publishing books? If so, there are various options available to you. And we want to help you find the best option possible.

I (Shelley) have to be honest. I am very thankful for self-publishing. I am also thankful for the continued advancements in how books are purchased and read. Years ago, you had to go into an independent bookstore to buy the books you wanted. Now, you can buy books online from Amazon.com, BarnesandNoble.com, Walmart.com, and the list goes on.

Not only that, but you can buy books electronically in various formats. I even have the Kindle app on my phone as well as a Kindle device that allows me to buy books and begin reading them in seconds. Talk about instant gratification! We can all see that times are changing in the world of publishing—and rapidly.

As the way we buy and read books changes, so does publishing.

- No longer is it necessary to submit your book to a long list of publishers and endure rejection after rejection.
- No longer is it necessary to invest thousands of dollars in self-published books that will sit in boxes in your garage for years.
- No longer is it necessary to pay a publisher money to self-publish your book (this is commonly known as a "vanity press").

Gone are those days. Say hello to eBook platforms and print on demand options for publishing print books.

Print on demand (POD) technology has changed the way print books are published. Instead of printing hundreds or even thousands of books and storing them in a warehouse, print on demand companies print copies of your book one at a time as your book is ordered.

Publishing Options

Self-Publishing

Definition: Self-publish your book on your own. You are the publisher and manage every stage of the process.

Quality: Good

Author's Risk: Low

Time to Print: Few Weeks

Author's Cost: Low – Moderate (pay for editing, formatting, book cover design, etc.)

Royalties: 10-70%

Potential for Income: Good

Control: Majority

Fulfills Print Book Orders: POD Publisher

Responsible for Marketing: Author

Independent Publishing

Definition: Self-publish your book through your own publishing company. You form your own independent publishing company, purchase your own ISBN, decide on what printer to use, and are responsible for every part of the publishing and marketing process. If you are interested in this option, we talk in-depth about how to form your own independent publishing company in chapter eleven.

Quality: Good to High

Author's Risk: Moderate to High

Time to Print: Weeks

Author's Cost: Moderate to High

Royalties: 10-70%

Potential for Income: Best (if successful)

Control: Total

Fulfills Book Orders: Author and/or POD Publisher

Responsible for Marketing: Author

Vanity Press

Definition: Publishes your book at your cost.

Quality: Good

Author's Risk: Moderate

Time to Print: Usually Months

Author's Cost: High

Royalties: Varies

Potential for Income: Low

Control: Moderate

Fulfills Book Orders: Author

Responsible for Marketing: Author

Traditional Publishing

Definition: Published by a commercial publisher who takes care of the entire process from start to finish.

Quality: Best

Author's Risk: Moderate

Time to Print: Usually 18 Months or Longer

Author's Cost: Varies

Royalties: 5-15%

Potential for Income: Low to Good

Control: Low

Fulfills Book Orders: Publisher

Responsible for Marketing: Publisher and Author. However, more and more traditional publishers are requiring that the author do most of their own marketing.

Now that you have a general idea of the different types of publishing options available to you, let's cover several steps needed to set up a solid foundation for publishing your book. After all, a solid foundation is the first step towards success.

PART ONE

Getting Started

CHAPTER ONE

Writing Your Book

Before you can self-publish your book, you first need to actually have a book. So it is only logical that the first chapter in a book on self-publishing be about writing your book. In the following pages we will walk you through doing some preliminary research, resources for writing your book, different ways you can write your book, and some other helpful writing related tips.

If you have already written your book, you may want to skip to the next chapter where we cover editing. Or, if your book is completely ready to go, you may want to jump to chapter three on building your marketing platform or even straight to part two where we get into the actual self-publishing process.

Preliminary Research to Do Before You Begin

Before you can start writing your book, more often than not, you are going to need to do some research. The type of book you are writing and how much you already know will determine just how much you will need to learn.

There are several things you need to know before writing your book. The two main categories I would break them into are facts and craft.

Facts

I (Heather) love reading historical fiction. There's just something... less stressful about things gone by. One of the biggest complaints I've seen in reviews from other readers in this genre is historical inaccuracies. If you are writing historical fiction, researching the time period is crucial. You have to know everything from what they ate to what they wore (and what they called it), and even how they talked, walked, and traveled.

There are resources for almost every time period you can think of for historical fiction authors. My old library had a whole section with monstrous books on time period clothing among other things.

Even if you are writing in modern day, it is important to check your facts. I read through a heated debated a while back in the comments section of an Amazon review where two reviewers were arguing about whether or not the main character (MC) should have been getting eggs out of a hen house on a snowy day.

Another example would be if you write a scene about a car breaking down and your MC has to take it to the mechanics to get it fixed, you need to make sure your symptom matches the diagnoses.

Facts matter. It's that simple.

Unless your work of fiction is based in a fantasy world, you need to make sure you have your facts straight. Take the time to do some research and make sure you are writing a believable story.

If you are writing fantasy, facts still matter, you just only have to worry about being consistent and true to what you have created. But consistency in your facts is still important.

If you are writing non-fiction, facts matter even more. Non-fiction authors are generally experts in their fields, so having factual errors can severely damage your credibility. And, depending on your niche, it could be detrimental to your readers if you have incorrect information or portrait an opinion as a fact.

What it comes down to is that, for the most part, it doesn't matter what you are writing, having your facts straight is a must. Then comes crafting the facts into a book worth reading.

Craft

Writing is an art. If you want to do well, you have to learn the craft. Most experts recommend writing every single day. The more you write, the better you will get. But it is equally important to study the craft of writing. On our blog, I have listed 6 books on our blog that I recommend for learning the craft of writing. You can find them here: www.trainingauthors.com/6-books-every-writer-needs

However, the craft of writing is about more than just learning to write. Crafting a fiction story is almost more important than having a story worth telling. I have read countless books that were well written that I cannot for the life of me remember what they were about, but I finished them (and probably left a decent review on Amazon). On the flip side, if the author could not craft the story in a believable or coherent manner, I probably put it down and/or left a negative review.

Learning to write takes work. Most people cannot just wake up one day and decide to write a book—at least not a good one. You will need to know about character development, plotting, point of view, story structure, and so much more.

Shelley wrote a post on our blog with six essential books for fiction authors (you can find it here: www.trainingauthors.com/6-essential-books-for-fiction-authors), but if you are writing a fiction novel, you'll need to do even more research than just those six books. If you want to succeed, you need to study and learn the craft.

While most non-fiction authors don't need to study plotting and character development, knowing how to craft a sentence, use correct grammar, and outline a book are all still important. Finding books to help non-fiction writers with their craft is much more difficult than finding books for fiction authors, but they do exist. You can find a list of books I recommend on our website here:

www.trainingauthors.com/6-great-books-for-non-fiction-authors

Additional Research for Non-Fiction Authors

Another thing that non-fiction authors should research ahead of time is their niche and target audience. Before you write a non-fiction book, you need to know that there is an audience for it. Who will read your book? Then, you should write it with them in mind. If you are writing a book for teens, you will want to know the way they talk, words they use, and examples they will relate to.

Non-fiction authors should know quite a bit about their market before they sit down to write their book. They need to know what their target audience has questions about or is interested in. Knowing your market beforehand will help you write a book they want to read.

I encourage you to take the time to do the research you need to write a great book with best-seller potential. Research really can make the difference.

6 Ways to Write Your Book

There is more than one way to write a book. I (Shelley) often hear authors say they do not know where to start when writing a book. Therefore, I am going to share six ways I have used to write a book to help you get started in the right direction.

#1: Write the Book Yourself

I know, I know. This is the most obvious option available. But, it is true.

You can simply sit down and write the book yourself.

However, it is often difficult to look at a blank screen or a blank piece of paper. That is why you may want to consider starting with a template.

I also like to conduct a brainstorming session where I write out an outline for my book. I really like using a mind map for my book outline because I can dump all my ideas into the mind map and then rearrange my outline until it is the way I want it to be.

However, I have also outlined books on scraps of paper while sitting in a restaurant with my husband. The important thing is to get your ideas onto paper (or a screen) so that you can start writing.

#2: Dictate the Book and Have it Transcribed

Another option for writing your book is to dictate the book and then have it transcribed.

This option works best for...

- Nonfiction books because fiction books tend to be more complex. However, fiction authors may want to try this method as well.
- Speakers who are more comfortable talking than typing. (Yep...this is me! I was a speaker before I was an author and am therefore very comfortable speaking.)

- Busy entrepreneurs, parents, etc. because you can record on the go with your mobile device.

If you use this method, I would still recommend starting with an outline before you speak your book. This will ensure that you have a solid plan for your book and that you stay on track as you speak.

I used this option for a couple chapters in my book, *"Body Image Lies Women Believe."* I had an audio transcribed and then edited it for the book. To be completely honest, the transcribed text did require a lot of editing. But I still found it helpful as it allowed me to write my section of the book much faster than starting from scratch.

There are so many ways to record audio. Here are just a few options to consider:

- On your computer using a microphone and the free software, Audacity.
- On your mobile device using a recording app.
- On a private teleseminar conference call where you call into via your phone and have it recorded.
- On your computer using dictation software like Dragon Naturally Speaking. I personally own this software and have used it to increase my productivity as well as decrease the strain on my hands and arms.

Transcription Service Sites

Over the years, I have researched transcription services and have listed several options below. Realize that prices are subject to change.

- Casting Words
  http://castingwords.com/
  $1.00/minute (budget) $1.50 (6 days) and $2.50/min (1 day)

- All Custom Content
  http://allcustomcontent.com/transcription.html
  $1.90 per audio minute* for Verbatim and Cleaned-Up Transcriptions.
  $2.20 per audio minute* for Fully-Edited Transcriptions.

- Transcriptions Plus
  http://transcriptionsplus.com/
  $1.50/minute (3-4 days)
  $2.50/minute (24 hours)

- Fiverr
  You can also find quality transcriptionist on Fiverr.com. Try them out for $5 and if you're happy, give them more work. Here are a couple current Fiverr gigs that have high feedback, but these gigs could change at any time:
  o $5 for 5 minutes: www.trainingauthors.com/ fiverr-5for5-translation
  o $5 for 10 minutes: www.trainingauthors .com/fiverr-5for10-translation

#3: Use a PowerPoint Presentation

If you are a speaker, you could use one of your existing PowerPoint presentations as an outline for your book. This was how our book,

"Forgiveness Formula" was written. My husband and I both had powerful presentations on the topic of forgiveness and decided to co-author a book on the topic.

One advantage of this option is that you can test your topic with a live audience to see how well it is received.

I won't lie...it still took a lot of work to put the content into a book format. However, it was well worth our effort! Plus, once our book was published, we were able to offer it at a merchandise table at our live events to help diversify our income.

#4: Hire a Ghostwriter

You can also hire a professional writer to write your book for you. They call this person a ghostwriter. You pay them a certain amount of money upfront to write the book for you. This way, you can put your name as the author, keep all the rights of the book, and keep all the future book royalties.

I have only used this option for one book and used someone I already knew. I was very familiar with her writing style, which made me confident in her ability to give me quality work. If you do hire a ghostwriter, make sure to get samples of their work and ask for references. You may also want to assign them several writing tests to determine the quality of their work.

You can find ghostwriters on Elance, writer's forums, and I have even heard of publishers that find quality writers on Craigslist.

#5: Organize an Anthology

Another option for writing a book is to organize an anthology. An anthology is a collection of short stories from various authors. In this case, you would only need to write an introduction, conclusion and possibly one of the chapters.

At the time of writing this book, my husband and I have published six anthologies. One example is our book for authors titled, *"Indie Author Book Marketing Success,"* which includes 14 chapters from 14 different book marketing experts. Therefore, I only needed to write one chapter. However, there is still work involved. I would call the rest of the process *project management.*

Here are a few steps required to publish an anthology:

1) Decide on a topic.
2) Create a page on your website that describes the project and include a form for authors to submit their work. You can also have a contract created that they sign to agree to your terms.
3) Recruit specific authors that would be a good fit for your topic.
4) Remind authors of the deadline.
5) Work on the other aspects of publishing a book. (i.e., choosing a book title, book cover design, editing the work submitted, formatting the book, etc.)
6) Communicate, communicate, communicate with your contributors.
7) Publish the book and begin the marketing process.

If you are really good at project management and networking with other authors and/or experts in your field, publishing an anthology may be a great option for you.

#6: Blog Your Book

Another option is to blog your book. This has been a popular option for nonfiction authors and was the method I used to write my first book. If you choose this option, make sure your chapters flow and are edited properly. Otherwise, you may get reviews stating it seemed like blog posts put together to publish a book. I would also recommend you add new information within your book that cannot be found anywhere else online.

3 Keys to Writing Success

There are several writing options available to help you get your book done, but making progress can still be difficult. And before you can publish your book, you have to finish writing it.

Many people are amazed that I have published 30+ books in various formats (print, large print, eBook, audiobook, etc.). To be honest, I am amazed as well! If you would have asked me when I published my first book in 2008 what I would be doing today, 5 years later, my answer would NOT have been *"working from home writing and publishing books and helping others do the same."* However, here I am doing just that.

And I love it.

But, it has not been easy. There have been many days I did not feel like writing, formatting, publishing, or marketing my books. There have also been many obstacles that I had to overcome.

This quote keeps coming to mind lately...

"Successful people do the things that unsuccessful people are unwilling to do."
- John C. Maxwell

And it is so true! There is a statistic that 80% of people want to write a book...someday. So many writers never reach their goal because they get sidetracked, stuck, or they quit. And that is why I want to share these three keys to writing success with you. I want to help you succeed in your writing and publishing efforts.

Key #1: Consistency

Being consistent is the key to success in so many areas of life. For example...

- Writing
- Spiritual growth
- Business
- Physical Fitness
- Etc.

I experienced this to be true in my life recently in regards to my physical fitness. I enjoy running for exercise but have not been consistent enough over the past few years to see much improvement. Within the last month, I finally listened to my husband and started running more consistently.

And something amazing happened...

I improved!

Plus, I started enjoying running again and have seen my race times get better.

In fact, as I was running this week, I realized that my "easy run" pace was my fast race pace just a few weeks ago.

I looked up my times and I set my current personal record (PR) for the 5k in 2006. I am getting close to it again and expect to set a new PR soon (even at elevation in Colorado) as long as I stay consistent. I did not ponder on it too long, but I was wondering this week where I would be today if I had stayed consistent with running back in 2006, over 7 years ago!

And the same is true for writing.

When you consistently write, you tend to get better and more efficient. Plus, you make forward progress on your book(s).

One way to stay consistent is to set goals. Write out your goals in your notebook or use a free online tool like Wunderlist.com. Make your goals specific and time oriented.

Key #2: Productivity

There are so many programs and books on productivity. We all want to get more done in the 24 hours we have been given in each day, right? It is so easy to get sidetracked online reading blogs, spending time on social media, and watching videos. I admit that one of my biggest time suckers is Facebook. I love connecting with my friends and family and yet it is so easy to spend hours scrolling through the feed and catching up with people when I should be writing. You might know the feeling.

One of the best tools for productivity is a simple kitchen timer.

You can also use our software, "Productivity Coach" (trainingauthors.com/productivitycoachsoftware) or a free online timer like Timer-Tab.com to increase your productivity dramatically by using a technique called time chunking.

Here is how time chunking works:

- Decide what you need to accomplish
- Close down your social media accounts, e-mail, Skype, IM, etc.
- Set the timer for 30 minutes
- Stay focused on that one task until it is completely done.
- If you need to extend it for another 30 minutes to finish the task, set the timer again.

I have used this technique often to get things done, especially tasks I keep putting off for another day.

Try it! I think you will be amazed at what you can get done when you really focus all your attention on that one task.

And give yourself rewards. When you meet a goal, find a way to reward yourself. It may be as simple as going for a walk with your dog, drinking a cup of coffee, or going on a shopping trip. Your reward can also be a 20 minute break to do whatever you want online.

Key #3: Accountability

Last year was filled with writing and publishing. And I got a lot accomplished. One of the things I credit to my writing success last year was having a writing accountability partner. I decided to ask another writer friend of mine if she would be interested in helping keep me accountable to with my writing goals and I could do the same for her. And she said yes!

We decided to form a private Facebook group to post our weekly goals and encourage one another. And it helped so much.

You can do this in so many ways: in person, via e-mail, through a private Facebook group, Skype, etc.

Resources You Can Use

There are tons of resources available for authors to use when writing their books. I (Heather) wanted to list some of the most helpful here, but you can find even more resources we use and recommend on our website at: www.trainingauthors.com/resources

Word Processors

Microsoft Word

Shelley and I both use Microsoft Word for writing our books. It meets all of our needs as authors and allows us to format our books for publication as well. I do know several authors who write and publish with the free Openoffice.org software that is comparable and compatible for the most part, so if you are on a low budget you might want to check it out.

Dragon Naturally Speaking Software

This is a voice dictation software that both dictates what you say and can enable you to control your computer with your voice. Shelley already mentioned in the section on speaking your book, but if your hands get sore, you do not enjoy sitting for long periods of time, or think best out loud, you can record portions of your book on an mp3 recorder or even an app on your phone, then have this program transcribe it for you. All you will be left with is the editing and polishing. Learning the voice commands to this program is essential if you want to use it on a large scale.

Project Management Tools

Evernote

If you keep a significant amount of notes for your book, this program will help you keep track of them. You can sign up for an account at: www.trainingauthors.com/evernote

FreeMind

Shelley and I use this tool for brainstorming our books. It is great for making notes and outlining your books. You can download this free software at: www.trainingauthors.com/freemind

Asana

We use this program to collaborate on projects, but you can also use it for giving yourself deadlines and planning out your to-do list for writing your book. Visit asana.com for more information.

Dropbox

A must-have if you are collaborating on any projects. This is great to use when working with an editor, cover designer, etc. on your book project as it allows you to save file folders that can be "shared" or accessed from multiple computers by invitation only. You can sign up for your free account at: www.trainingauthors.com/dropbox

Scrivener

One of the best tools we can recommend is Scrivener. It allows you to outline and write your book, keep notes, and so much more. It's designed to help you easily manage large writing projects in one location. It's like a word processor and project management tool combined into one program. Shelley uses it for fiction writing, but it can be great for non-fiction books as well. However, this is not a free program. You can see all the products they have available at: www.trainingauthors.com/scrivenerproducts

Once you have your book written, you have only completed the first hurdle towards becoming a successful author. Your next step is editing it. If you are ready to learn about the editing process, turn the page to start the next chapter, Editing for Success.

CHAPTER TWO

Editing for Success

Poor editing detracts from the reader's experience, and it also can cast you in a bad light as an author. Needless to say, good editing is a huge part of being a successful author. After all, knowing what punctuation to use, knowing proper grammar and other rules is the first step to self-editing your work.

In this chapter, we're going to cover five steps to self-editing your writing, but first, I (Heather) wanted to share a few editing resources that I have found helpful.

Recommended Editing Resources

The Chicago Manual of Style

If you really want to know the right answers when it comes to editing, the *The Chicago Manual of Style* is the way to go. If you are a Christian author, I also recommend *The Christian Writer's Manual of Style*, as it covers many aspects of Christian writing that are not covered in *The Chicago Manual of Style.*

<u>Grammar Girl</u>
I use this website frequently when I am stumped on anything related to editing. In fact, usually if you Google any grammar, punctuation, or other editing question, at least one link will most likely point back to this site. It is simply an amazing resource. Mignon Fogarty, a.k.a. Grammar Girl, also has a number of books available on Amazon that would make great references to keep on your desk. (www.quickanddirtytips.com/grammar-girl)

<u>Author's Quick Guide to Editing Your Book</u>
This book is a gem. Kristen Eckstein covers tips for self-editing, common mistakes, and the different types of editors you can hire to edit your book. If you are new to editing, I highly recommend picking up a copy of this 99 cent eBook (you can read my full review of it on our blog: www.trainingauthors.com/the-ultimate-challenge-for-authors).

5 Steps to Self-Editing Your Writing

Once you have a firm grasp of grammar and know what to watch for, you are ready to start self-editing your book. On the next page, you will find the five step process that we recommend. Good editing can take time, but it is definitely worth the effort.

Step #1: Take a Break

The first step to take when self-editing your writing, is simply to step back and take a break. Work on something else for a while to clear your head. This gives you a breather, but can also help separate you from your writing and help you see it with fresh eyes when you come back to it. You will catch more mistakes if you take a break.

Step #2: Use Computer Software

It sounds simple, but actually clicking the button in Microsoft Word to run the spell check can catch editing errors you might have missed. If you have a subscription to any editing software, running it can help catch things you might miss on your own.

Examples of computer editing software include:
- Grammarly: www.trainingauthors.com/grammarly
- AutoCrit: www.trainingauthors.com/autocrit
- Edit Your Novel: www.trainingauthors.com/edityournovel
- etc.

Step #3: Read Backwards

Start at the end of your book and work your way back to the beginning one sentence at a time. Reading what you have written out of order can help you distance yourself from what you meant to say and get a better look at the structure of what you actually wrote.

Step #4: Read It Aloud

Reading your writing out loud is a great way to check the flow of your writing, but it also can also catch a ton of other editing mistakes. You can read it aloud to yourself, have a friend read it to you, read it to a friend, or even record your book in audio format and kill two birds with one stone.

Step #5: Rinse and Repeat

Self-editing takes time. It's a process. And it is a process that should be repeated more than once. Traditional publishing houses send each book to at least 3 editors, and each editor usually looks at it more than once. And even those books still have typos and other edits that slip past everyone. Going through the self-editing process multiple times, can help you catch more mistakes.

Optional Step #6: Print It

Something I have personally found helpful is to print it out. I always catch more typos after I print something. I don't, however, recommend printing it before going through the above process at least once or twice. You can waste a lot of paper that way. Only when you think it's completely perfect should you print it. After you print it, go through the first four steps again. You might be amazed at what you find.

The Next Step...

Even after thoroughly self-editing your writing, we still recommend getting a pair of professional eyes on your book. It is extremely hard to catch mistakes that you have written, no matter how many times or different ways you go through something. And as the author, going over and over and over it can actually tempt you to change things that don't need to be changed or second guess your wording.

As I mentioned earlier, publishing houses usually have at least three different editors look at each book, so getting another pair of eyes is always a good idea. However, by self-editing your book before you send it to an editor, you can save yourself both time and money. Self-editing may take time, but going through edits that someone else sends back can take even more time, and you also have to factor in the time the editor has your book while they work on it.

No matter how you publish your writing, editing is an important step to take. You can find a list of the editors we recommend on our website at: www.trainingauthors.com/recommended-outsourcers-for-authors/#editors

Different Types of Editing

Before you can hire a professional editor for your book, you first have to know what kind of editing you are looking for.

It is important to note that different editors describe various types of editing differently. You might have an editor who classes developmental editing under ghostwriting, or who offers both proofreading and copy editing services. I will list them here just to give you an idea of the different options, but you will want to check with any editor you are considering as to what their editing entails.

The four main types of editing are:

Proofreading or Copy Editing

Some editors will call this a light edit as it usually is not very in depth. These editors expect to see books that are already close to perfection. They look for typos and grammatical errors. Their job is to check for consistency and accuracy—that is it. They may point out places that do not flow well or other content errors, but they do not try to fix them, and they may not even point them out as it is not part of their job.

Line Editing

This is often referred to as a heavy edit or a content edit. It is where the editor goes through your book looking at the sentence structure, flow, and even the content to make sure it is complete and factual. It costs a bit more than the regular copyedit or proofread.

Line editors will usually catch typos and grammatical errors as well, but they often recommend getting an additional copyedit or proofread after you have finished their suggested revisions. How in depth and complete a line edit is will depend on your editor.

Ghostwriting

Ghostwriting can mean two different things. You can hire someone to ghostwrite your entire book from scratch (as Shelley mentioned in chapter one), or you can send them your finished book and have them polish it for you. When going the second rout, they should send you back a book that is ready to be formatted and published.

We recommend using caution and diligence when working with a ghostwriter. You are essentially giving them complete control of your book. They will re-write sections and sentences to make them sound the way they think they should, add sections and sentences for clarification, and even delete or move sections and sentences that are out of place.

The appeal to using a ghostwriter is that it is less hands-on. You send it off and it comes back ready to go. You do not have to worry about approving edits or sifting through comments when you receive it; it is done.

You do, on the other hand, lose control of your book. It is important to remember that your book has your name on the cover, not theirs, and it will represent you as an author. If you hire a ghostwriter, we highly recommend at least reading the final product before clicking "Publish."

Developmental Editing

This is a like a cross between ghostwriting and line editing. These editors will make the changes like a ghostwriter will, but they will track them in the document and you can go through and approve or reject them. Some editors refer to this as a substantive or structural edit.

What to Look for in a Professional Editor

Before hiring an editor, there are several things you will want to look at and ask about before agreeing to work with them. We recommend check their websites for these things before even contacting someone. However, not every editor will have all of this information on their website, so you may need to contact them and ask direct questions.

Editing History

Check for the types of books they have edited. Editors that edit fantasy might not be the best choice for historical fiction (or nonfiction). Nonfiction editors may not be the best choice for children's books. Some editors are versatile, others are not. So check their history to see what genre(s) they work in the most.

You will also want to know how seasoned they are. The more books they have edited, the more experienced they are. Experienced editors have a process and usually know what they are doing. Most authors will recommend hiring a seasoned editor.

However, hiring a newbie editor can be a great way to save money. Just know that they won't catch everything, and may require some training. You also won't want to pay as much for someone with little to no experience.

Pricing

How much an editor charges will vary depending on their experience, workload, and several other factors. The more satisfied clients they have, and the higher their workload, the more likely they are to charge more. However, just because someone charges an arm and a leg does not mean that they are worth it. We recommend looking for someone in your price range and making your decision based on that.

Most editors will either list their prices by cost per word or cost per page. An editing page is 250 words. So if they are charging $2.50 per page, it would be 1 cent per word. Based on these prices, if you have a 75,000 word book, it will cost you $750 for editing.

The Editorial Freelancers Association has more information on pricing on their website if you want a better idea of industry rates You can find that at: www.the-efa.org/res/rates.php

Description of Editing Process

As I said earlier, different editors classify editing differently. Look for what each edit includes, how they track it, and how they work. Do they go through it once, twice, etc.?

What this comes down to is you want to know what you are paying for. Knowing how in-depth their process is can help you decide between them and another editor that charges the same amount.

Contacting an Editor

After you have an editor that looks good on paper, you are ready to initiate contact with them. When you get in touch with them, we recommend digging deeper to get the full picture of what working with them will be like. Here are a couple of things to watch for:

Response Time

How long does it take them to respond to your inquiry? If it takes a week or two for them to get back to you, chances are that they are either swamped and do not really have time for a new client, or they are not very reliable or dedicated.

Grammar

It is harder to catch errors in your own writing than in someone else's. However, if an editor's e-mail to you is filled with grammatical errors and typos, they probably don't have an eye for editing. Many editors will take the time to proofread their e-mails before hitting send, but even if they are too busy to take the extra time on each inquiry, they should at least display a good grasp of grammar in their responses.

Before agreeing to work with someone, you will want to consider asking them about the following:

References

Can they give you a list of other authors they have worked with so you can contact them? This will let you know if the other authors were satisfied with their work.

Sample Edit

One of my editing friends says, "any editor worth their salt will offer a sample edit." This is where you send them a chapter or certain amount of pages from your book, and they edit it (free of charge) and send it back.

Always, always get a sample edit before making a commitment to an editor. This lets you see how they edit with a real life example. You will get a feel for how they work on your book and it will give you a good idea on whether or not you will work well together.

Having someone return an edited book where they completely destroy your writing style is never a fun surprise. Getting a sample edit beforehand can eliminate wasting time and money on an editor who sees things completely different than you do.

Personal Preferences

If you have any personal preferences in your writing style that you want them to know about, ask them ahead of time if they are okay with that. It will save you both times in the long run if they aren't marking something as wrong that you intended to be that way.

One example is the word "okay." I always write it out, whereas Shelley uses the short form, "OK." Both are grammatically correct (and "O.K." would be, too). Having an editor mark each usage wrong would be a huge waste of time on a personal preference, but I have heard of it happening (www.quickanddirtytips.com/education/grammar/ok-okay). Whatever forms you use, they should be used consistently throughout your book.

Communication

How you prefer to communicate will make a big difference on whether or not you are compatible with an editor. If you prefer e-mail and they want to have weekly phone consults (or vice versa), that could be an issue. Ask them how often they will check in, how they prefer to be contacted, etc. This will give you an idea of what to expect.

Turn Around Time

This is huge. You must know how long they will be working on your project. I always ask for two weeks to a month earlier than when I actually need the project done. This provides a cushion of time in case they are late for some reason. Remember, you will also need time to go through their edits, and having it back early will give you more time to do that.

When Approving Edits...

Remember, editors do not always know best. You can absolutely question them and/or over rule them—it is your book. When you are sifting through edits that your editor has sent back, feel free to question them, get a second opinion, or even do some of your own research to check grammar rules.

I once had an author tell me that she questions her editor on a regular basis. If they cannot tell her exactly why they recommended a change, she writes it off and leaves it the way she originally had it.

I have personally had edits come back that would make sense if I approved them, but the suggested changes would also alter the original meaning to something new. At times like that, you need to look at your original word choice to see if you can clarify your meaning, or just ask a few other people to read the paragraph to see if they are confused as well. I often post my questions like this in a Facebook group for authors. The others in the group all chime in and let me know if I actually need to make changes.

CHAPTER THREE

Building Your Marketing Platform

I f you are new to self-publishing (which we will assume you are since you are reading this book), you may not be aware that book marketing is a huge part of being an author. There are millions of books available to readers, so if you want them to notice yours marketing will be required.

We believe that it is never too early (or too late) to start marketing your book. In fact, the sooner the better. If you are looking to traditionally publish your book, one of the first questions an agent will ask is if you have an online platform/following. I actually have an author friend who walked into a meeting with a book publisher at a writing conference and was offered a book deal based solely on the fact that her website ranked #1 on Google for the keywords in her niche.

Building a marketing platform for your book is extremely important.

Whether you want to self-publish your book or seek out a traditional publishing contract, having a platform will give you someone to market your book to as soon as it is released. And, if you have a platform, you can generate some pre-release excitement and build suspense by sharing your progress, doing a cover reveal, etc.

Before you start building your platform, you will want to do some research (I know, it is a recurring theme in this book, but research is important). There are two main things you will want to research: Target Audience and Keywords.

Target Audience

Knowing who will buy your book will help you set up and define your marketing campaigns. For example, if you write for women, Pinterest could be huge for you, whereas if your target audience is male, that might not be the best place for you. I've often heard it recommended to set up an ideal reader profile. Write down how old they are, male/female, where they like to hang out, other books they like to read, movies they like to watch, favorite pastimes, etc. Doing this will give you a better idea of how to market your book and where to spend your time.

You will also want to narrow down your niche and determine the demand for your book. If you are unfamiliar with the word "niche" it is the specialized area that people want to know about. When people ask you what your niche is, they want to know exactly what you write about.

Here are three niche examples:

- Crockpot cooking
- Passive Income Generation
- Christian Living

Keywords

Once you know what you are writing about and who your target audience is, the next step is to do some keyword research. Keywords are words that people often search for when looking for books on your subject. If you write fiction, this won't be as in depth for you, but it is still important. Fiction keywords are more genre and setting oriented; e.g., romance, historical, WWII, Victorian Era, etc. Non-fiction keywords will be more topic or target audience oriented. For example, if you were writing a cookbook, your keywords could be crockpot, recipes, beef, or other words that relate to your book. Or you might single out your audience; e.g., busy moms, recipes for kids, etc.

Once you have some ideas for your keywords, you can use research tools to help you determine which ones will get you the best results when marketing your book. Google has a free keyword research tool that you can use if you have an AdWords account (also free). You can find it here: adwords.google.com/KeywordPlanner

Other options include:

- www.keywordeye.com
- www.keywordspy.com

- www.semrush.com

Keywords help readers find you in search engines. You will use them on your Website, in hashtags on Twitter and Facebook, and even on Amazon. We will talk more about websites in a moment, but I do want to note that if you have a website through SBI (Site Build It!), their keyword research tool can't be beat. They also offer it as a Word-Press site add on. You can find more about it here: www.bizxpress.com

5 Steps to Building Your Platform

I love checklists. They always help me make sure I have everything done and keep me headed in the right direction. So I wanted to share my 5 step checklist to building a solid book marketing platform:

#1: Create a Website or Blog

Shelley and I highly recommend having your own website. You can get affordable hosting with Bluehost, or more robust hosting through Servint. Another option would to go with an all-in-one company like SBI—however that is a bit more expensive.

Author websites are important as they are sort of like a base of operations for all your marketing efforts. You will want to include the link to your website in the back of your books, on your Facebook page/profile and Twitter accounts, on your business cards, etc. Having a good author website is key to successful book marketing in my honest opinion.

We use and recommend using WordPress themes for your website, and have a tutorial on how to set them up on our blog at: www.trainingauthors.com/building-an-author-website

#2: Register for Google Plus

Google Plus is great for authorship, search engine results, and so much more. You can learn more in this article from Copyblogger: www.copyblogger.com/google-plus-authority.

And you can sign up for your free account here: plus.google.com

#3: Set Up an E-Mail List

Having a list of dedicated followers who you can send updates to can really help take your success to the next level. Shelley and I used to use Aweber to manage our e-mail lists, but decided to switch to Traffic-Wave. They are one of the most affordable options we have found. However, we do highly recommend both companies. You can read our post about why we switched here: www.trainingauthors.com/aweber-vs-trafficwave

#4: Create Key Social Media Accounts

When setting up social media accounts, it is always best to know who your target audience is and where they hang out. You will need to do the research to see what platforms are the best for your niche, but we've listed the two that we think every author should have below:

Facebook

Every author should have a Facebook page. Facebook has over 500 million users. Creating a page is quick and easy, and it's a simple way for fans to connect with you. Even if all your FB page does is send your readers to your website, it's worth having.

If you need help setting up your Facebook page, here's the link to a training we recommend: www.trainingauthors.com/facebook

Warning: Facebook can be addictive. Check out this post Shelley wrote with 5 steps to get back the time Facebook is stealing from your writing for time saving tips: www.trainingauthors.com/5-steps-to-get-back-the-time-facebook-is-stealing-from-your-writing

We also want to note that while we recommend having a Facebook page, we don't think having a different page for each book is necessary. One Facebook author page will give you a way for your fans to connect with you, without taking up too much time to update and manage.

Twitter

Twitter technically beats out Facebook with over 650 active profiles. However, with Facebook, you're only allowed to have one account, and multiple pages, with Twitter you set up a new account for each profile you want. So even though Twitter registers more profiles, that doesn't mean that it has more users. It is active though and it would be a good idea to create a profile.

You can learn more about Twitter in the following posts here on our blog:

- How to Write an Effective Book Tweet
  www.trainingauthors.com/how-to-write-an-effective-book-tweet
- 40 Hashtags for Authors
  www.trainingauthors.com/40-hashtags-for-authors

Or, if you need even more help getting started, we recommend this training course by the Savvy Book Marketer:
www.trainingauthors.com/twitterguide

#5: Set Up a Gremln Account

Gremln is a tool we use to help automate some of our tweets. Twitter is very fast paced, and none of us can be on 24-7. To comp for that, we use Gremln to pre-schedule recurring tweets to market our books.

Important Note: This is not the only way we use Twitter and is not a replacement for the real thing. It is merely a tool to increase exposure.

Through Gremln, you can schedule tweets to recur automatically every so often. We don't recommend repeating the same tweet more than once or twice a month. Most of our tweets are scheduled every 21-45 days. But we do have some that recur yearly during the holidays or on other special dates.

We also use HootSuite to schedule some of our posts, but Gremln is the only one that allows recurring tweets. And we think it is best for scheduling evergreen tweets that promote your book.

We will share some more about marketing your book in the conclusion, but we wanted to make sure you knew that marketing your book is important—and the sooner you get started the better!

A Word of Caution

As an author, your most important job is writing. Marketing gets you noticed, but without having books for readers to buy, it is pointless. Before you start marketing your book, we recommend deciding how you will divide up your time.

Doing research beforehand will help you get better results with less time and effort than just winging your book marketing strategy. Decide how much time you want to spend marketing your book, and then decide how you can make the most of that time. As we mentioned earlier, you can download our free training, Building a Book Marketing Plan, when you sign up for our newsletter here: www.trainingauthors.com/newsletter

PART TWO

Self-Publishing Your Book

CHAPTER FOUR

Pre-Publication Decisions

Before you can publish your book, there are several decisions you will need to make. In this chapter, we will cover choosing your book title, pricing your book, categories and keywords, and how to write your book description.

Book Title

How Do You Choose a Book Title?

That is the question a friend asked me (Heather) a few weeks back. And it is actually a really good question, so I wanted to share my 6 step process here. But first, I wanted to cover what makes a good book title.

A Good Book Title is...

Relevant - Good book titles let the reader know what the book is about all on its own.

Emotional – A good title will either play on the reader's emotions or their desire for more information.

Unique – The best titles are original.

Choosing A Book Title That Sells

Here is my 6 step process to choosing a book title that sells:

Step #1: Know What You are Working With.

You have to start with some basic knowledge about your book and your niche so you can choose a relevant title. I recommend asking yourself what the message of your book is. A good title should reflect that.

Step #2: Do Some Research.

Check for relevant keywords. You can use keyword tools to see which keywords are generating the most interest online, and even how much competition there is for them.

You can also check out what other authors in your niche are using for titles–which ones are selling the best. I'm not suggesting you copy any of them, but they can give an idea of what works. You need to be creative, but informed creativity is not just creative, but clever.

If you want to get more information on how to choose a book title that sells, here are a few other articles that I recommend:

- Writing Good Book Titles
  www.trainingauthors.com/writing-good-book-titles
- How to Title Your Book
  www.rachellegardner.com/2010/03/how-to-title-your-book
- 4 Things to Keep in Mind When Choosing a Title for Your Book
  blog.karenwoodward.org/2013/05/4-things-to-keep-in-mind-when-choosing.html
- How to Write Magnetic Headlines (for blogging or non-fiction)
  www.copyblogger.com/magnetic-headlines

Step #3: Brainstorm.

I recommend having a brainstorming session (with your research close at hand) where you come up with at least 20 titles. Not all of them have to be good, but sometimes the best titles come from combining two or three.

You can also enlist beta readers or your Facebook following to help. One of the authors I follow online shared the synopsis for one of her new books and shared a title she liked, then asked for suggestions. She got an outstanding response and some great ideas.

Step #4: Narrow it Down.

Once you have several you can choose from, narrow it down to just 3-5 of your favorites.

Step #5: Do More Research.

Once I have narrowed my list down to just a few book titles that I really like, I always check on Amazon to see if there are already books by that title. Titles are not protected by copyright laws, but remember how I mentioned the best titles are unique? If someone is searching for your book, you want them to find yours, not a dozen different books to choose from.

I also like to run my title ideas through a trademark checker. Even though titles cannot be copyrighted, if an author has an entire series, they can trademark it. I use: www.trademarkia.com

This is also a great time to interact with your following. You might poll them to see which one they like the best, or post one and ask them what they think the book will be about (this only works if you have not already shared about your book online).

Step #6: Make Your Choice!

After you have the results from all of your research, you should be able to make a choice and choose a title that will represent your book well and help it sell. On occasion, I get to step #5 and realize the route I have been going does not work for my following and decide to start

SELF-PUBLISHING BOOKS 101 | 59

over. If this happens to you, know it is not time wasted, but a wise decision that will continue to pay off for years to come.

How to Price Your Book

A common question that authors ask us is, *"How should I price my book?"* There is a lot of great advice on this topic and the answer can vary greatly depending on your niche and your goal.

Three Foundational Keys for Publishing Success

Before we dive into the topic of pricing strategies, I (Shelley) want to give you a few key reminders that we have already covered in this book. I know this information is basic and should be a given for any author, but over and over again I see authors skipping one of the steps below. In order to see success with your book sales, there are a few foundational things I assume you already have in place.

1) You have written a good book.
2) You had your book edited.
3) You had an eye-catching book cover designed (we will cover this more in chapter 5).

I encourage you to not skimp on any of these three steps when publishing your book.

Why? Let me explain...

A great book will sell the rest of the books in your series. A mediocre book may not.

A book that has NOT been edited may get torn apart by reviewers. Reviews do tend to influence sales; therefore, getting a bunch of bad reviews due to poor editing is not good for the success of your book sales.

And finally, your book cover is the first thing your potential customers will see. It is your first opportunity to make a good impression and encourage them to find out more about your book. If your cover screams "amateur author," many readers will immediately click off your book sales page. You will not only lose a book sale, but you may also lose a potential long-term fan.

If you do not have these basic foundational keys in place for your book, no matter what you do with your pricing strategies, you will struggle to have success.

3 Things to Consider When Pricing Your Book

1) Research Other Books Within Your Niche.

Doing some basic research of other books within your niche allows you to see the average price for other books similar to yours. This does not mean you have to price your book at the same price as your competitors, but it does give you information about what your target audience is willing to pay.

2) Know How Much You Will Get Paid in Royalties for Each Price Point.

For example, KDP currently pays book royalties as follows to self-published authors:

- $0.99 to $2.98 = 35% royalties
- $2.99 to $9.99 = 70% royalties
- Above $9.99 = 35% royalties

Therefore, the "sweet spot" for pricing your books tends to be between $2.99 to $9.99 so you can earn 70% royalties. If you want to price your book lower than $2.99, $0.99 is usually the recommended price as $1.99 tends to not sell as well. However, you will need to do your own testing to see what price point is best for you.

3) Understand the Minimum Price Allowed for Your Print Book.

With print books, there are more overhead costs. Therefore, there is often a minimum price at which you can price your books. For example, CreateSpace will give you this information when you publish a book in their system. This "minimum price" goes up significantly if you use their expanded distribution. If you want to lower the price of your print book for a promotion, you cannot lower it beneath that minimum price.

If you are not sure how to change the price of your print book, Heather has written a tutorial on our website to help you here: www.trainingauthors.com/how-to-lower-the-price-of-your-paper-back-book

2 eBook Pricing Case Studies

Pricing Strategy #1: Lower Book One to $0.99

The first strategy we will cover is to lower the first book in your eBook series to $0.99. Why $0.99? Well, $0.99 is an impulse buy price point. Most readers are willing to risk $0.99 on a book from an author that is new to them. And if they like your book and writing style, there is a good chance they will be willing to invest a little more money in the other books in your series.

A Real Life Case Study Example

I love knowing what really works. Not just theory, but what is truly working for authors in their book marketing strategies. Therefore, I want to share an example of an author who uses this pricing strategy successfully.

Lynnette Bonner has priced the first book in her Christian Historical Romance series, "*The Shepherd's Heart*" at $0.99. She has then priced the rest of the books in the series at $3.99. Since she dropped the price of book one to $0.99, it has remained consistently below an Amazon rank of #2000 overall. In addition to the first book selling well, the other three books in the series have also had increased sales and are ranking below #10,000 or so on Amazon.

Previously, Lynnette priced the first book at $3.77 and the rest of the books in the series at $5.77. Since lowering her prices, her overall royalties have increased.

<u>Pricing Strategy #2</u>: Offer Book One for FREE

There are so many opinions on offering your eBooks for free. Many authors balk at the idea because of all the time and energy they put into writing and publishing their books. They feel they deserve to get paid for their work. I understand, I totally get it.

However, what if lowering the first eBook in your series to free could actually increase sales for the rest of the books in your series and increase your overall monthly royalties? Would it be worth it to you?

A Real Life Case Study Example

One author, Lindsay Buroker, believes that offering the first book in her fantasy series, "*The Emperor's Edge*" permanently free has increased her fan base as well as the sales of the other six books in her series.

Lindsay has blogged about her success and shares 5 reasons to consider giving an eBook away free (www.lindsayburoker.com/book-marketing/5-reasons-to-consider-giving-away-a-free-ebook). She has also experienced increased international sales as a result of her first book being free on Amazon UK, Apple overseas stores and other international eBook stores (www.lindsayburoker.com/tips-and-tricks/how-do-you-improve-international-ebook-sales).

Will These Same Strategies Work For You?

The only way to know if these pricing strategies will work for you is to test them on your book series and then track your results. With book marketing, it is always important to track the success of the strategies you implement.

I also recommend starting a weekly book sales spreadsheet to track your book sales. This will allow you to track trends in your sales and know what is working and what is not. Amazon will give you monthly sales data, but I think it is helpful to track your sales a little more closely.

Some authors I know actually track their sales on a daily basis. That is a little too much work for me, but I do recommend tracking your sales on a weekly basis.

Book Description

Another important pre-publication decision you need to make is what you will post for your book description. This will show up on your sales page and is often what helps readers decide if they will buy your book.

Several considerations when writing your book description:

- Try to hook your reader with the first sentence.
- Describe what the reader will get out of the book.
- Create an emotional connection with the reader.
- Include endorsements or reviews from high profile people in your niche.

- Add a call to action. This step is optional, but one we have used for several of our books. One example of a call to action is, "Scroll up and click buy to start reading this book now."

I will admit copywriting is <u>not</u> one of my strengths. That is why I love Ken Envoy's book, "*Make Your Words Sell.*" He makes writing sales copy simple to understand and apply - without feeling forced to be too "sales-y." He keeps it real.

Oh, did I mention he now gives his book away FREE? Yep!

No more excuses for poorly written headlines and book descriptions! Before you know it, you'll be writing a headline and description for your book that draws people in like a magnet.

You can download your free copy of "Make Your Words Sell" at: myws.sitesell.com

After finishing the book, force yourself to sit down and write out your book description. I recommend setting aside at least 2-3 hours of *uninterrupted* time to complete this step.

Fiction authors may be interested in reading Joanna Penn's blog post on how to write a book blurb here: www.thecreativepenn.com/2010/11/16/how-to-write-back-blurb-for-your-book

Categories and Keywords

Another pre-publication decision you need to make is what category you will choose and which search keywords you will enter for your book.

For example, you are able to choose 2 categories and 7 search keywords when you publish your eBook via KDP. There are even certain keyword requirements in order for your book to be classified as certain categories. You can find out more here: kdp.amazon.com/help?topicId=A200PDGPEIQX41

For print books published via CreateSpace, you can choose 2 categories and 5 search keyword terms. Here is more information: authorcentral.amazon.com/gp/help?ie=UTF8&topicID=201231280

I like to choose one category where there is not much competition and one category where there is a lot of demand. You will want to make sure that the categories you choose fit your book well and make sense. Otherwise, you may attract readers outside of your target audience.

Step #1: Go to Amazon.com, choose "books" and press "go." If you are researching categories for a Kindle eBook, then choose "Kindle Store" from the dropdown menu and then click on the Kindle eBooks link on the left hand side.

You will then see a list of book categories in the left hand column. Start your search by clicking on the categories that fit your niche.

Step #2: Try to get as drill down as specific as you can within a category. Some categories have niche subcategories that are less competitive and easier to rank in. You can see the number of competing books in parenthesis after the category title.

Step #3: Now it is time to choose your categories. You can choose up to two for each book. Obviously, the less competition there is the better. For my less competitive category, I try to choose categories with less than 2000 competitors whenever possible.

I share in much more detail how to choose categories in my book, Marketing Your Book on Amazon: 21 Things You Can Easily Do for Free for Increased Exposure and Sales. Find out more at: www.trainingauthors.com/books/marketing-your-book-on-amazon

3 Things to Put in the Back of Your Book

When writing your book, one thing to consider is the content you will include in the back of your book.

This is major "real estate" within your book that you can use to connect further with your readers.

Here are three simple things you can include in the back of your book:

#1: Opt-in URL to Your E-mail List

You do have an e-mail list, right?

If not, I highly recommend you start a targeted e-mail list of readers as this has been my most successful book marketing technique.

Once you have an e-mail list, I recommend putting a link to your opt-in page at the back of your book. I usually offer something free I think my target audience will be interested in as an ethical bribe to encourage them to sign up for my list.

Let me give you a couple of examples of how I add a link to my opt-in e-mail list in the back of my books.

For my books for authors, I include a blurb like this:

Sign up to our exclusive newsletter and get access to our author's training ($27 value) for FREE at the link below. You will get access to our PDF training, templates and more. Plus, you will never miss out on new tutorials, tips and updates! You can sign up here. (Hyperlink the last sentence, or include the link.)

I also write Christian non-fiction books and use this blurb in the back of my books:

Love getting FREE Christian books online? If so, sign up to get notified of new Christian book promotions and never miss out. Then, grab a cup of coffee and enjoy reading the free Christian books you download. You will also get our FREE report, *"How to Find Free Christian Books Online"* that shows you 9 places you can get new books...for free! Sign up here.

I now have thousands of targeted readers subscribed to both my author list and my Christian book list. I then set up an autoresponder series that automatically goes out to each new subscriber to continue building a relationship with them.

You can sign up to my list to get an idea of how I set up my autoresponder messages. Then, when I have a special book promotion, I send out an e-mail broadcast to my list about it, which almost always yields good results.

For fiction authors, you can simply create a "New Release Mailing List" and include something like this in the back of your book:

> To hear about my latest books first, sign up for my exclusive *New Release Mailing List* here: Your URL goes here.

OR

> Want to find out what happens next? The next book in my series will be released later this year. Sign up to my mailing list to be the first to know when it is out. Your URL goes here.

#2: Blurbs for Your Other Titles

Another option you can include in the back of your book is information about your other book titles. This is especially helpful if your book is part of a series. You can include an excerpt of the next book in the series along with links to buy it.

I have done this with my book series on gratitude. After sharing an excerpt of the book "21 Prayers of Gratitude," I then include this call to action:

> This was an excerpt from the eBook,
> *"21 Prayers of Gratitude:*
> *Overcoming Negativity Through the*
> *Power of Prayer and God's Word."*
> Read all 21 prayers for only $0.99 here (hyperlinked).
> Prefer print?
>
> A compilation of all three books in the series,
> "A Life of Gratitude" makes a great gift.
> Get the paperback version of the entire series here (hyperlinked).

You can take this technique a step further and include links that you can track. You can do this through HootSuite's ow.ly links, bit.ly links, or the Pretty Link Lite plugin for WordPress. You can create a specific link to include in your book so that you can track the number of clicks that you get. This will help you to know if including an excerpt in the back of your book is an effective marketing technique for you.

#3: Short Note Requesting Reviews

We all know that getting reviews is helpful for sales. More and more readers (myself included) are starting to depend on reviews to help them decide if they want to buy a book. However, getting reviews can be tough.

One way to encourage reviews is to add a simple request at the back of your book. All you have to do is ask. Here is an example from the back of K.M. Weiland's books (fiction and non-fiction):

Note From the Author: Reviews are gold to authors! If you've enjoyed this book, would you consider rating it and reviewing it on www.Amazon.com?

You can also replace the link to Amazon with the direct link to your book's listing.

CHAPTER FIVE

Book Cover Design 101

Even though designing a book cover can be relatively simple, you should put some thought into it and consider hiring a professional. Your book cover design <u>will</u> make the first impression to your potential readers. It could scream, "Amateur!!" or it could invite them to find out more.

According to the Wall Street Journal, the average person shopping in a bookstore spends 4 seconds looking at the cover and 14 seconds reading the back cover. Therefore, you need to design your cover to draw people in and write the headline and the description to sell.

If you are like me, you might be asking, "How do I do that?" Good question! Here are a few suggestions to help get you started.

Book Cover Design 101

Brainstorming Ideas

A great way to brainstorm ideas for your book cover is to browse the Amazon.com book store online. You can also go to your local book store and look at a variety of book covers to get ideas.

Another way to research ideas for your book cover is to use bookcoverarchive.com. This website allows you to quickly browse many book covers at once and will even tell you which fonts were used for the covers you like.

To get some ideas of good book covers, check out the previous winners of Joel Friedlander's eBook Cover Design Contest.

What to Include When Designing a Book Cover

Front Cover:
Think of your front cover like the billboard advertising your book. It must be done well to draw people to take a second look at your book. The front cover of your print book can also be used when publishing your book as an eBook. If you are publishing an eBook only, you will only need to have the front cover designed.

For both the eBook and print book cover, make sure that it looks good in a thumbnail version as well. When your target audience is searching the internet using their computer or mobile device, they will see a very small image of your book. Does your cover still look good at a size of 160 pixels high x 100 pixels wide? Is the title still readable at the smaller size? These are all considerations you should take into account when designing your book cover.

For the front cover (and eBook covers), include the following:

1) Title
2) Subtitle
3) Author's name
4) Related picture or drawing**

**Important: *Make sure you buy pictures that give you the rights to use them commercially. Read the fine print. You can check out fotolia.com for stock photos or search "stock photos" on Google.*

One mistake many self-published authors make is they put "by Author's Name" on their cover. You should not include the word "by" but only include the author's name on the cover.

Spine:
Beware of too much clutter on the spine. Keep it simple with an eye-catching headline and the author's name.

1) Title
2) Author's name

Back Cover:
The back cover is the most complex, but also very important (second to the title). Remember, people spend almost 80% of their time reading the back cover when shopping for books.

1) Title
2) Description

3) Benefits and Highlights (bullet points are recommended for non-fiction)

4) Endorsements for your book (up to three quotes)

5) Author's biography

6) Author's picture

7) Barcode/ISBN

Specifications for Book Covers:

Make sure you know the requirements for the book cover for your publisher. For example:

- KDP recommends the size of your cover art have an ideal height/width ratio of 1.6. This means a minimum of 625 pixels on the shortest side and 1000 pixels on the longest side but for best quality, your image would be 1563 pixels on the shortest side and 2500 pixels on the longest side. (Reference: kdp.amazon.com/help?topicId=A2J0TRG6OPX0VM)

- CreateSpace requires that all print covers be 300 dpi resolution. They all list their book cover requirements on their site here: www.createspace.com/Products/Book/CoverPDF.jsp

- ACX requires that the cover art be no smaller than 2400 x 2400 pixels at 72 dpi resolution. (Reference: www.acx.com/help/rights-holders/200474610#cover-art-specs)

- Smashwords requires that all eBook covers be at least 1,400 pixels wide. (Reference: blog.smashwords.com/2012/06/new-ebook-cover-image-requirements.html)

- Apple (iBookStore) requires that all eBook covers be at least 1,400 pixels wide. (Reference: blog.smashwords.com/2012/06/new-ebook-cover-image-requirements.html)
- Barnes & Noble Nook recommends (recommends, not a requirement) a minimum height of between 1,200 to 2,000 pixels. (Reference: blog.smashwords.com/2012/06/new-ebook-cover-image-requirements.html)

Methods for Designing Your Book Cover

Choose One of the Methods Below to Create Your Book Cover:

You can design your own book cover using...

- Your publisher's book cover software (free, but has fewer options and is only provided by certain publishing companies)
- A book cover template (must have Photoshop software, also takes time and skill)
- Book cover software (must purchase software and has a learning curve)
- Or hire a professional (most expensive and must find a designer you like)

If you want to hire a designer, but do not know who to trust, consider crowdsourcing sites like 99 Designs and Crowdspring. Simply name your price, post your project and then watch as graphic designers bid on your job. The best part? Love your book cover design or get your money back!

We also recommend Killer Covers, where you can get a quality cover designed for only $117 for eBooks and a print book cover for $447. Find out more at: www.trainingauthors.com/killercovers

Sometimes you can find a great designer on Fiverr.com. However, you may need to hire several designers to get the concept and quality you want. I usually search by rating to sort the gigs by the best designers.

We also list some outsourcers you can hire on our website here: www.trainingauthors.com/recommended-outsourcers-for-authors/#bookcover

CHAPTER SIX

Self-Publishing
Print Books

Are you interested in self-publishing print books? If so, we have researched several options for you to consider below. But first, here is a list of items to consider when choosing a self-publishing option for your print book.

- Reviews and reputation among other writers
- Upfront publishing fees
- Royalty payment structure and when you get paid
- Author's cost to purchase additional books for resell
- Contract terms (i.e., do you keep all rights to your cover and interior, copyright, etc.)
- Cost of any additional services (cover design, editing, marketing)
- ISBN number and barcode included
- Listing on Amazon.com and other online retailers

Options for Self-Publishing

Option #1: Use an Independent Publishing Service

Some authors simply want someone else to manage their book project. In this case, you will pay more to have your book published, but you will not have to invest the time into managing outsourcers, budgets, deadlines, etc.

I personally know the owners of both of the following services, have researched them fully and am confident that if you use either service, you will end up with a quality book. In both cases, you will still be the publisher, they are simply handling all the details for you (i.e., hiring outsourcers for book design, editing, formatting, etc.).

Ultimate Book Coach

Kristen Eckstein of Ultimate Book Coach offers independent publishing services. You can find out all the details here:

www.trainingauthors.com/recommended-outsourcers-for-authors/#kristen

She also offers a digital course on publishing print books called, Self Publish on Demand. You can find it here:

www.trainingauthors.com/selfpublishondemand

Believers Press

Believers Press is an excellent option for Christian authors. You can see the services they offer, pricing and more here:

www.believerspress.com/publishing-options

Option #2: Self-Publishing

If you are willing to put in the time and effort to learn how to publish a quality book, there are several affordable self-publishing options available. Each option below offers print on demand services. This means that when a book is ordered, it is printed. This eliminates the need for stocking inventory, which lowers your overall costs. You only pay for what you need.

CreateSpace

CreateSpace is a company owned by Amazon that offers authors the ability to self-publish print books.

Standard Distribution
- Amazon.com 40% of list price
- Amazon Europe 40% of list price
- eStore 20% of list price

Find out more details about royalties here:
www.createspace.com/Products/Book/Royalties.jsp

Expanded Distribution

Expanded distribution is now free, but previously cost $25. This changed after Ingram Spark was launched (see below).

For the expanded distribution, there is a 60% of list price for all options below.
- CreateSpace Direct
- Bookstores and Online Retailers

- Libraries and Academic Institutions – Must have a CreateSpace-Assigned ISBN

More about expanded distribution here:
www.createspace.com/Products/Book/ExpandedDistribution.jsp

ISBN Options via CreateSpace
- CreateSpace-Assigned ISBN FREE
- Custom ISBN $10 (can only be used with CreateSpace)
- Custom Universal ISBN $99
- Buy your own Universal ISBN from MyIdentifiers.com

Details about CreateSpace ISBN's here:
www.createspace.com/Products/Book/ISBNs.jsp

Sign Up
You can sign up for a free account here:
www.trainingauthors.com/createspace

Ingram Spark

Ingram Spark is a service provided by Lightning Source for small, independent authors and publishers.

Fees/Revenues
$49 set up fee (waived if you order 50 books within 60 days)
$12/year per book

From the research I did, there seems to also be a $40 fee every time you need to update your file, but I recommend verifying that with Ingram Spark.

40% or 55% discount (The author makes 45% or 60% minus printing costs.)

More on Ingram Spark's Fees and Revenues:
www1.ingramspark.com/Portal/CostsandRevenue

ISBN Options
You do have to buy your own ISBN when you publish through Ingram Spark and can do that through MyIdentifiers.com. Here are the current costs for ISBN's:
> 1 for $125
> 10 for $250
> 100 for $575

I recommend you check out their FAQ page here:
www1.ingramspark.com/Portal/FAQ

Lightning Source

Lightning Source is another option available and is a step up from Ingram Spark with more options available. I have heard it is harder for independent authors to get approved for a Lightning Source account unless you have at least 20 titles. But, you can always try.

<u>Sign Up</u>

You can sign up for an account ($49 set up fee) here: www1.ingramspark.com/Account/Signup

Book Print on Demand

Book Print on Demand is a print on demand publishing service for authors and publishers.

<u>Fees/Revenues</u>

- No set up fees and no additional cost to change your files.
- Low printing costs that are competitive with CreateSpace.
- You only pay for printing costs and shipping.

Get a custom quote for your book here: bookprintondemand.com/pricing

<u>ISBN Options</u>

You do need to buy your own ISBN when self-publishing books through Book Print on Demand and can get them at: MyIdentifiers.com.

From their website: "Publishers only need an ISBN number if they are planning on selling a book at retail. This includes Amazon.com and other online retailers. If a publisher or author is only publishing a book for family, friends, conferences or direct-to-consumer distribution purposes, they do not need an ISBN."

Expanded Distribution Available

Book Print On Demand can offer expanded distribution, sometimes called Print-to-Order (PTO) gives you distinct advantages: your product data to thousands of retailers, including B&N, Books-A-Million, Baker & Taylor, Ingram and all of the Christian trade (Family, Life-Way, Mardel, CBD, etc.). This expanded distribution is available through their Anchor partnership and you can find out more details here: www.believerspress.com/distribute/global-distribution

Or you can contact them for more details here: bookprintondemand.com/contact/

Here are a few of the details of this distribution program:

- Set up is $249 for the first title, and $149 for subsequent titles in the line.
- Annual renewal for each title is $99.
- Distribution fees are 30% of net revenue. This fee includes all costs that would normally be charged separately, including storage, handling, returns, accounts receivable, and any free freight with qualifying orders. Actual freight costs are billed to the author/publisher and should be offset by the consumer shipping charges.

Ecommerce Option

This is a very unique service and allows you to sell your books directly from your website or Facebook page.

- They print your book as it is ordered and ship it to your customer for you. Therefore there is no inventory that you need to stock and no shipping on your end.
- There is an initial set up fee, but can be a great business model for authors as it is the way to collect the most royalties from your book from any option I have researched. The only fee is a 15% gateway fee (plus printing/shipping costs).
- All sales are done through your own PayPal account. Therefore, you need to collect sales tax and shipping costs.

Get all the details about their ecommerce option here: bookprintondemand.com/ecommerce

I also recommend finding out more about Book Print on Demand at their FAQ page here: bookprintondemand.com/faq

Sign Up
You can sign up for a free account here:
app.bookprintondemand.com

Option #3: Use a Combination
Did you know that you can choose more than one option? As long as you have a universal ISBN, you are able to distribute your book using all three options mentioned above in the self-publishing section.

For example, you can use CreateSpace to publish your book on Amazon, Ingram Spark or Book Print On Demand to distribute your book to bookstores via the Ingram catalog, and Book Print on Demand to buy copies for live events and sell books from your website.

Also, if you have previously published on Amazon with a CreateSpace ISBN, you can purchase a new universal ISBN and publish the same book through IngramSpark in order to get your books in book stores. Therefore, you will have your book published through CreateSpace and IngramSpark at the same time with different ISBN's. This way you can keep your book published with the CreateSpace ISBN on Amazon so you don't lose your sales momentum.

Here are some articles on how to use multiple options:

Amazon and Lightning Source by Joel Friedlander
www.thebookdesigner.com/2011/09/amazon-and-lightning-source-the-end-of-an-era

Plan B by Aaron Sheperd
www.newselfpublishing.com/blog/#planb

How Do I Get My Print Book into Bookstores?

The first question many first time authors ask is, *"How do I get my book in bookstores?"* To be very honest, retail (bookstores) is not where I recommend most authors start and here's why:

- It is expensive – you have to give 40-55% of your profit right away.
- It is very competitive – there are thousands of titles competing with your book.
- It works best when there is already a demand for you book and you have built your book marketing platform.

52% of books are sold online. Therefore, I recommend that you start by selling your book in online bookstores first. Once you have built a platform and have success selling your book at a local or regional level, then you can consider distribution to bookstores on a national level. Otherwise, you may spend a lot of time pursuing something that yields very little return on investment (ROI).

Other Considerations

Set Up Pre-Orders for Your Print Book Before the Launch Date:

We personally have not taken pre-orders but Eric Van Der Hope, a co-author our book, Indie Author Book Marketing Success, has. He describes how he takes pre-orders on Amazon in chapter 5 of our book here: www.trainingauthors.com/books/indie-author-book-marketing-success

There are multiple options available to authors who wish to pursue self-publishing their print books. You no longer have to fill your garage full of books, go into debt, or hand over all of your rights to a traditional publishing house. You can self-publish your book!

What I Use

When I decided to self-publish my first book, I researched many options. I did not have a huge budget (or any budget, really) and so I was looking for the best quality publishing for the lowest price. I ended up choosing CreateSpace to publish most of my print books and here are some reasons why listed below.

Through CreateSpace, you can:

- Publish your book with no upfront costs (you will need to pay for editing, formatting, and book cover design).
- Open an account for free - no hidden costs.
- Add a new book title to your projects and fill in all the book information yourself, which gives you complete control.
- Upload your interior book template and book cover files by the click of a button.
- Get an ISBN number and barcode for free. However, I do recommend that you purchase your own ($10 CreateSpace ISBN or Universal ISBN).
- Quick turnaround allows you to publish your books fast. I have published my books from start to finish in as little as one week!
- No revision fees.
- They offer both matte and glossy finishes for your cover. Personally, I think that the matte finish looks more professional for most books.
- Set up your own personalized store front at CreateSpace for free to sell your books online.
- Set the selling price of your book and change it whenever you want for special promotions.
- Sell your books 24/7 (literally, while you sleep) and CreateSpace handles all the order processing and shipping for you!
- Choose direct deposit or a mailed check for your monthly royalties from online sales. I like direct deposit because I get instant access to my earnings.

- Order books at your cost to sell in person and ship them to your home, all at cost price. Book Print on Demand also offers prices similar to CreateSpace for buying books at cost.
- Set up special discount codes for certain sales or groups.
- Have your book listed on Amazon.com for free.
- Sell your books on Amazon.com - these orders are eligible for super saver shipping (with $35 minimum purchase, restrictions apply), one-day shipping and 1-click ordering.
- And much more!

The Down Side to CreateSpace?

- Every really good thing still has some negatives. Let me share a few about CreateSpace with you.
- To sell with CreateSpace, you need a US Individual Taxpayer Identification Number (ITIN). Therefore, if you live overseas, this step may delay your publishing date.
- If you want to print a hardcover book, you will need to look elsewhere. Currently CreateSpace only distributes soft cover books.
- If you want a very small booklet or a full color book, the cost might be better with other publishers. Shop around first.
- If you want to sell internationally, you may want to look into Ingram Spark as the royalties for international sales with CreateSpace are not very good.
- If you want to sell your book in bookstores, CreateSpace is not the best option for you. See the previous section for more details.

- And finally, keep in mind that CreateSpace is a print on demand publisher and may not be the right fit for you.

However, if you want a quick, easy and cost-effective way to get published, go for CreateSpace.

Timeline for CreateSpace Self-Publishing

I have found through my experience, that it can take as little as one week to self-publish a book through CreateSpace. So, if your book is already written, you could be making money by selling your book in person, online at your own webpage, and on Amazon.com by next week.

Here is how the timeline usually works:

Day 1: Create your account and upload your files.

Day 2: Wait for CreateSpace to approve your files. Make any necessary changes, if needed, and re-upload your files. (Note: If you re-upload your files, you start the process over at day one. So follow their guidelines from the beginning to avoid any delays.) Once your files are approved, order your proof copy.

Day 5: Your proof copy comes in the mail. This is a great feeling to see your book in print form for the first time! Celebrate and enjoy the moment. Then, examine your proof copy and, if satisfied, approve your proof copy. (Note: Shipping time will vary depending on your shipping address.)

Congratulations! Your book is now ready to start selling on your CreateSpace webpage.

Day 7-14: Your book will now be visible and ready to sell on Amazon.com with search inside features. This step varies, sometimes it is live within a few days; sometimes it takes up to one week to be live on Amazon.com.

Congratulations: It is now time to start marketing your book and selling copies!

Formatting Your Book for Print

If you want to self-publish your book, we recommend to start with a self-publishing book template. I have developed my own, but there are also free templates available online that you can download and use. Actually, it is really simple. Let me share how I designed my template and give you links to download more book templates for free.

When I decided to self-publish my first book, I did not know where to start.

So, I started doing some research and realized most authors simply type their book in a Microsoft Word document and then convert it to PDF to upload to their publisher. It sounds simple, but I wondered how to format my Word document so that it would be the correct size for printing.

That is when I developed my own book template.

Designing Your Own Self-Publishing Book Template

My book template is simple—nothing fancy. But, it works. And I continue to write and sell books today using my original template.

So what did I do?

1) First, I opened a Microsoft Word document and saved it to my computer. If you don't have Microsoft Word installed on your computer you can also use the free OpenOffice.org software.

2) I then researched the fonts that are recommended for print books—the best fonts for titles and for the text—and inserted them into my template. I set up my first chapter in the fonts and sizes I decided upon.

3) Next, I resized my Microsoft Word document to: 8.5 inches x 5.5 inches. It is simply half of a regular sized sheet of paper (8.5 inches x 11 inches) and tends to be the most popular and most affordable size to print a book.

4) Then, I created an endorsement page, a title page, copyright page, table of contents page, and dedication page.

5) And finally, I was ready to start writing my book in my self-publishing book template.

After I was finished setting up my first template, I saved it as a template that I now use over and over for all my books. It really makes writing new books a snap because I already have my template ready to go!

Add Pizzazz to Your Template

To spice up the design of your template, you can add tables, text boxes, graphics, and more. Pretty much, if you can design it in Microsoft Word, you can add it to your book template.

I have decided to publish my book interior in black and white to save money in publishing costs. But, if you want full color, you can publish in full color. Just realize, it <u>will</u> be a lot more expensive.

Tips on Inserting Graphics

One thing you need to know about inserting graphics into your Microsoft Word template is to choose graphics that are 300 ppi (pixels per inch) for print quality. I choose to buy stock royalty free photos from istockphoto.com which gives you the rights to use the pictures on printed materials, like books. You can search for images on their website. Once you find the image you want for your book, make sure to download it in the correct size for your book in 300 ppi quality.

Istockphoto.com will show you what file size and quality you will get, so make sure to get it right. Otherwise, your pictures could turn out fuzzy and look unprofessional in your book. It pays to make sure you get the right size the first time—I know this from experience!

Once you download your photo and insert it into your template, you can then change it to black and white (or grayscale) as well as add text to it in Microsoft Word. Or you can use graphic editing software like Adobe Photoshop.

However, Photoshop is expensive if you don't already have the software. So, another great option is to use free graphic editing software.

Free Graphic Editing Software

Here are a couple options I have used and recommend. You can also search Google for many other options.

- Picasa – a downloadable program for editing and organizing photos. Can also be used to edit and share photos online.
- Photobucket - an online photo manager with free editing and hosting tools.

Pixlr.com is another online graphic editor that you can use, however we have not used it personally.

Want to See the Template I Designed?

Well, you can!

And it's even free—because my goal is to help <u>you</u> get published.

Download my template and begin using it today for free when you sign up for our free newsletter. Through our newsletter, we will share with you the tips and tricks we have learned regarding publishing and marketing books.

We love to share what we have learned with others—and that is what this book, our website, and our newsletter is all about!

So, sign up now and download for free my self-publishing book template (.doc) here: www.trainingauthors.com/newsletter

Download More Free Book Templates

However, you may want to publish your book in a different size. And if you do, CreateSpace.com offers many different template sizes for you to download for free. They have templates available to download in the following sizes:

5 x 8 inches

5.06 x 7.81 inches

5.25 x 8 inches

5.5 x 8.5 inches

6 x 9 inches

6.14 x 9.21 inches

6.69 x 9.61 inches

7 x 10 inches

7.44 x 9.69 inches

7.5 x 9.25 inches

8 x 10 inches

Check Out CreateSpace Book Templates Here:

www.trainingauthors.com/createspace-templates

Download Professionally Designed Book Templates

If you would like to use a professionally designed template, we have used and recommend Book Design Templates. They have eBook and print templates designed in Microsoft Word that you can purchase and use for your books.

Get professionally designed templates here:
www.trainingauthors.com/booktemplates

How to Convert Your Book Template to PDF for FREE

Most book publishers, like CreateSpace, will want your final book draft uploaded to their website as a PDF document. PDF is simply the acronym for *Portable Document Format*. It is the most common format used for eBooks and document downloads because it maintains the formatting of your book or document on any operating system and between various versions of software.

Adobe Acrobat is the gold standard for PDF conversion and your best bet to guarantee the best quality for your book.

However, the Adobe Acrobat 9.0 standard edition currently has a list cost of $299. Many times you can find it cheaper on Amazon or Ebay, but if you are on a shoestring budget like me, then $300 is a big chunk of change.

Therefore, I researched all the free PDF conversion software to find another viable option for self-publishing books. And I found one: PDF995.com, which is what I use to save my book template as a PDF file.

Technically you can upload a Microsoft Word file to CreateSpace, but I have not found it to be as accurate as uploading a PDF file. You can also save your Microsoft Word file as a PDF, but it still seems to cause errors when uploading to CreateSpace. Therefore, I still recommend using PDF995 as outlined below.

Easy Steps to Covert Your Book Template to PDF

Why pay lots of money for software to convert your book template to PDF when you can do it for free? Right?

There are many different types of free PDF conversion software available, so it should be easy. However, it is not as easy as it looks. That is because you need to save your PDF in the same size your book will be printed. Most free PDF conversion software does not allow you to customize the page size. But, the good news is I found a way! It is possible with PDF995 when you are publishing a book that is 5.5 x 8.5 inch size.

Here's how:

1) Download PDF995 software and install it on your computer
2) Create your self-publishing book template in Microsoft Word as 5.5 x 8.5 inch size (download mine for free by signing up at: www.trainingauthors.com/newsletter).
3) Choose File, then Print
4) Once the print screen opens, choose PDF995 from the drop down menu of printers
5) Click on the properties button

6) Then, click on the advanced button

7) In the advanced screen, choose "Statement [5.5 x 8.5]" from the dropdown menu for paper size

8) Click "OK" three times

9) Choose where to save your PDF document and press save

10) If using the free version, an advertisement will then pop-up. To make this go away, you can pay $19.95 for the full version.

11) Congratulations! Your book is now saved in PDF format for the 5.5 x 8.5 inch size and ready to upload at your self-publishing company of choice.

Discover When You Need an ISBN for Self-Publishing

Most likely you are familiar with this acronym: ISBN (International Standard Book Number). But, what is it really, why do you need one and where is the ISBN lookup found?

The ISBN is commonly confused with a barcode. However, the ISBN is not the barcode. It is simply what it says it is... a number.

When you do an ISBN lookup or ISBN number search, you simply type in the assigned 10 or 13 digit number to get the book title, author and publisher. Pretty slick, huh?

When Do Self-Publishers Need an ISBN Number?

So what is an ISBN number and why do you need one?

The ISBN number is an identifier used world-wide and continues to be the standard for identifying books internationally. In short, you could say that the ISBN number is an _identifier._

It identifies the title of the book (print, audio, electronic, etc.) that is either published or self-published and also identifies the book's publisher. Therefore, if a bookstore wants to order a particular book, the ISBN number allows them to contact the publisher and place an order. It is also helpful to the publishers for tracking orders and sales for a particular book.

If you plan on selling your books in stores, libraries or with wholesalers, then you need an ISBN number. However, if you plan on selling your books on your own, an ISBN is not required.

According to ISBN.org, you are to issue a new ISBN number for the same book published in different ways.

For example, you will need a new ISBN number for:

- Each updated edition of your book
- Each different version of your book (audiobook, PDF, electronic, etc.)
- Each language the book is written

If you made minor changes to your book and reprint it, no new ISBN number is needed.

Should You Use the ISBN from the Publisher or Get Your Own?

It's really up to you whether you use an ISBN that is provided or purchase your own. The ISBN simply identifies the publishing company. If you want to be listed as your own publisher, then you will need to buy your own ISBN.

Read the fine print with your publishing company. If you are not comfortable using their ISBN, then most of the time you can use your own.

You can buy ISBNs in blocks at the US ISBN agency's website, Myidentifiers.com.

Where Do You Put the ISBN?

Make sure you place the ISBN on the copyright page of your book as well as the back cover.

If your publisher places a barcode on your book for you, like CreateSpace, then you don't need to worry about the back cover. If you need a barcode made, you can have it done at the US ISBN agency's website, Myidentifiers.com or do a search online for other barcode providers.

What Does An ISBN Look Like?

You may see ISBN numbers that are both 10 digits and 13 digits long. Why? Well, ISBN numbers were 10 digits for over thirty years. Then, on January 1, 2007 the official ISBN system changed to 13 digit numbers. Therefore, all new ISBN numbers are now 13 digits long.

If you bought your ISBN prior to the switch, don't worry. You can get yours switched over by using the converter at ISBN.org. However, you <u>cannot</u> change your number by simply placing three digits in front of it. It must be properly converted.

Unfortunately, once a book is published with a certain ISBN, that number can never be reused.

What items are <u>not eligible</u> for ISBNs?

- Advertising materials
- Blogs (ISBNs are not assigned to items updated frequently like blogs, magazines or online databases)
- Board games
- Calendars
- Music CD's (ISBNs are only assigned to audio book CD's or instructional CD's)
- Clothing
- Coffee mugs
- Electronic newsletters
- Video games
- Emails
- Food/medicine
- Magazines, academic journals or other periodicals
- Online databases
- Pictures/photos (ISBNs are used only for text, never for pictures)

- Playing cards
- Sheet music
- Software (ISNBs are only used for educational software)
- Toys
- Websites

Publishing Large Print Editions

Did you know you can publish a separate print book that is a large print edition on CreateSpace? When you publish a large print edition, it will then be linked with your Kindle, print and audiobook versions. I have done this with my book, "A Life of Gratitude."

Although we have not had many sales of our large print books, one author told me that 50% of her sales are of the large print edition. It is another way to provide your book to your readers and potentially diversify your income.

How to Publish a Large Print Edition of Your Book

I contacted CreateSpace about publishing a large print edition book and here is what they said:

"You will be required to set up your title as you would any other using the large font size (i.e., at least 16 pt font).

Under the 'Description' of the Distribution section you will need to indicate that this is a large print book. Once this box is ticked, your title will be listed as 'Large Print' on the Amazon detail page.

Furthermore, you will need to set up your book as a new title with a new ISBN. In addition, your large print title will be linked with the paperback and Kindle version if they offer the same content."

Conclusion

Therefore, all you need to do is change the size of your font, check the formatting for any changes, and finally upload the changes as a new book.

Amazon has an entire separate section for just large print books that you can see here: www.amazon.com/Large-Print-Books/b?ie=UTF8&node=300950

Printing Hardcover Editions

With CreateSpace, there is an option to order hardcover copies of your book to sell from your website or at live events. However, they do not currently offer hardcover distribution.

If you are interested in this option, you will have to contact CreateSpace support directly to request this option. They will then create a hardcover version of your book from your paperback printing files within 1-2 weeks.

Currently, the Hardcover Upgrade includes a one-time setup fee of $99 per title and you can select 60# white or cream interior paper and the following binding options:

- Case-bound laminate – hardback book where the cover image is printed, laminated and bound directly on the boards that make up the cover of the book

- Library Cloth with Full Color Dust Jacket – hardback book with a durable, navy cloth cover and a detachable, printed outer cover

Once the Hardcover Upgrade service is complete, you will be able to order hardcover copies at a wholesale rate, which includes fixed and per-page charges. The fixed charge for each copy is $6.50 and an additional $2.00 for the library cloth with dust jacket option. The per-page printing charge is $0.015 for a black and white interior. If the book has any color images or text within it, the book is considered full-color and the per-page printing charge is $0.15.

.

CHAPTER SEVEN

Self-Publishing eBooks

We have been successfully publishing our own eBooks for years, and have researched several options we have not tried as well. In this chapter, we will share some of the different options that are currently available, ISBN requirements, how to format eBooks, and the pros and cons of DRM.

eBook Publishing Options

There are many ways to self-publish an eBook. You can publish it on Amazon, sell it from your website, or use another platform to publish your book. We live in a digital age. There are interactive book apps for phones, digital story books for kids, and new ways for publishing eBooks are being invented all the time. In this section, I (Heather) will outline the three main ways for authors to publish eBooks. If you are interested in publishing outside the box, you might find this book on designing your own book app helpful: www.amazon.com/dp/B00BMH1KJK

If you write comic books, Kindle has a comic book creator that helps you turn your comic into an eBook. You can find out more about it here: www.amazon.com/gp/feature.html?docId=1001103761

Self-Publishing eBooks Directly to Each Platform

Here are a few platforms we recommend publishing your eBook to directly:

- Amazon Kindle Direct Publishing: kdp.amazon.com
- Barnes & Noble Nook: www.nookpress.com
- Apple's iBookStore: itunesconnect.apple.com/WebObjects/iTunesConnect.woa/wa/bookSignup

Most authors (not all) report Amazon being their #1 income generator and we have seen this to be true for us as well. When publishing your book directly to each platform, you have to learn the formatting requirements of each company and keep different files for each format.

Using eBook Distributors

Instead of publishing your book directly to all of the individual platforms, you can choose to go through an eBook distributor such as Smashwords. Many of these options are available with no upfront fees, but they do keep a portion of the book royalties. On the up side, you only have to format your book once, and they will re-format it for the other devices for you. It is a great time saver, but does cut into your royalties some.

We use Smashwords to distribute our books to the majority of eBook retailers. We do publish directly to Amazon through KDP, but have our books sent to Barnes and Noble, the iBookStore, and Kobo through Smashwords distribution. What we really love about Smashwords is their ability to use 100% off coupons. Of course, if you wanted to publish directly to all the platforms, you could still upload your book to Smashwords to use solely for that purpose.

You can learn more about publishing on Smashwords in our "Get Your eBook Done!" course for authors. Find out more here: www.trainingauthors.com/ebookpublishingsuccess.

Other options for eBook distribution would include Draft2Digital, and BookBaby. There are others, but those are three options.

Selling Your eBook From Your Own Website

Many authors prefer to sell their eBooks from their own website. You can sell the PDF version, a .mobi copy, an .epub file, or any combination of the three so readers can chose their preferred reading method. An easy way to do this would be to use a third party such as My eBook Master, but you can also set up shopping cart and file management systems on your own.

You can find a tutorial for My eBook Master on our website here: www.trainingauthors.com/easily-sell-pdf-ebook

Shopping cart options include:

- ClickBank
- PayPal
- eShop (for WordPress sites)
- And many more.

For file hosting, we use and recommend Amazon S3, but you can also research others before deciding what is best for you. When hosting your eBook files, it is important to make sure that they are protected. We currently use Amember (www.trainingauthors.com/amember) to protect our download pages and links, but you can also use a S3 cloak/expiration plugin, or, again, research other options.

ebooks and ISBNs

It is easy to get confused when it comes to ISBNs and eBooks. As Shelley mentioned in the last chapter, ISBN stands for International Standard Book Number and each edition of your book needs a different ISBN so that it can be identified. However, when it comes to eBooks, they are allowed to have ISBNs, but not all of them require it.

Here's what I mean:

Kindle eBooks use ASINs - these are provided free by Amazon to every Kindle eBook and this is the number used to identify them. No ISBN is required.

Nook eBooks use BN IDs - again, these are provided by Nook to every Nook book and is what they use to identify books. No ISBN is required.

iBooks used to require an ISBN, but recently removed that requirement. They do still encourage it though, and recommend buying one from Bowker.

Smashwords does still requires an ISBN to use when publishing through their expanded distribution channels. They will provide you with a free one or allow you to use your own.

To top all of that off, all of the platforms allow you to use an ISBN if you choose. You would have to purchase these on your own, and, if you chose to do so, you would need a different ISBN for each edition of your book. That's one for the .mobi Kindle edition, one for the Smashwords .epub, a different one if you publish your .epub directly to Barnes and Noble, etc.

Formatting, Templates, Software, and Outsourcers

One of the biggest parts of publishing your eBook is the formatting. A poorly formatted book will lead to bad reviews and low readership. Readers can preview your books formatting with Amazon's "Look Inside" feature or by downloading a sample to their Kindle, so it really can make or break your book sales. This chapter would not be complete without some formatting advice, however it would take an entire book to cover it all.

If you are good at following guidelines, you can pick up the formatting guides free from most eBook platforms and distribution companies. I have listed two of the main ones below:

Kindle:

www.amazon.com/Kindle-Direct-Publishing/e/B008241EAQ

Smashwords:

www.smashwords.com/books/view/52

Nook allows you to upload your file and convert it to an .epub within their system. You can then make any formatting changes you need to and check the layout. Or you can use an ePub converter like www.2epub.com and convert it to an .epub file prior to uploading.

If you are looking for a comprehensive guide, we have a tutorial on formatting and publishing eBooks. It includes the Microsoft Word template we use, video tutorials, and more. You can get it here: www.trainingauthors.com/ebookpublishingsuccess.

Here are some other formatting and template options:

Joel Friedlander's Book Templates – While we use our own templates for most of our publishing needs, Shelley has used Joel Friedlander's templates for Children's eBooks (you can watch her video tutorial about it on YouTube at: www.youtube.com/watch?v=WV_-61kWvpE), and we used one for the print version of this book. He also has templates that you can use to do both the print and eBook versions of your book, and we highly recommend them. You can find out more at: www.trainingauthors.com/booktemplates

Having a book template can give your eBook a professional look and really help it to stand apart. Templates are not a formatting end, but do get you started in the right direction. Once you have one, you will need to format your book within the template.

Kinstant Formatter – If you are looking for a simple solution to formatting your Kindle eBooks, check out Kinstant Formatter. Shelley has used them and recommends them for an affordable solution. www.trainingauthors.com/kinstantformatter

Scrivner - Scrivner is another formatting option that many authors use for eBooks. Kristen Eckstein has some great templates for Scrivner formatting available here: www.trainingauthors.com/scrivner

Formatting can take a lot of work, so another option would be to outsource it. You can also find a list of outsourcers we recommend for formatting eBooks on our website here: www.trainingauthors.com/recommended-outsourcers-for-authors/#bookformatting

The Pros and Cons of DRM

What is DRM?

DRM stands for Digital Rights Management and according to KDP it is "intended to inhibit unauthorized access to or copying of digital content files." (Reference: kdp.amazon.com/help?topicId= A36BYK5S7AJ2NQ#3-13)

This is one of the decisions you must make when your first upload your Kindle book via the Kindle Direct Publishing (KDP) dashboard. It is important to note that once you publish your book, this decision regarding DRM cannot be changed.

Now that we have covered the basics of what DRM is, let's discuss the pros and cons of DRM and enabling it on your Kindle eBooks.

Pros of DRM

The main advantage to enabling DRM on your eBook is that is adds an extra layer of protection to prevent unauthorized sharing of your copyrighted work. However, enabling DRM will not stop all piracy. There are ways to strip the DRM from the eBook. Therefore, the "bad guys" you are trying to keep out can still find a way to remove the DRM.

For some authors, enabling DRM on their eBooks is one way they can protect their copyrighted work. They do not like the thought of someone stealing from them and will do anything they can to prevent it from happening.

Cons of DRM

Unfortunately, what often happens with DRM is that it penalizes the customers of your book. Many readers like to have access to their digital books on multiple devices. However, DRM can prevent them from having access to the book they bought on non-Kindle devices.

This can be annoying to the customer and may even result in lost book sales as some readers will refuse to buy books that are DRM enabled.

I (Shelley) heard this analogy about DRM and thought it made the point well. Enabling DRM is like placing a lock on your book. However, this "lock" keeps the honest people (i.e., paying customers) out.

It does cause anyone who is dishonest to work harder to remove the "lock." But in the end, it does not truly stop piracy.

Other Considerations

Personally, I do not enable DRM on my Kindle eBooks. I want to make it as easy as possible for my customers to access and read my books. Choosing to not enable DRM may also help the messages of my books reach more people and positively impact more lives.

And ultimately, piracy is not the problem for most authors—obscurity is!

Therefore, if your book does get shared by your customers, consider it as one form of marketing. Who knows, you may even develop some new readers and fans as a result.

Ultimately, as the author, the decision is up to you.

You must do your own research and decide what options will work best for you and your books. If enabling DRM helps you sleep better at night, go for it. But ultimately, the disadvantages appear to out-weigh the advantages.

Self-publishing eBooks is a great opportunity for authors. There are multiple options available and it's easily customizable to each authors goals.

CHAPTER EIGHT

Self-Publishing AudioBooks

Have you thought about creating an audiobook version of your current book(s)? Some people prefer listening to audiobooks rather than reading them. Therefore, you may be missing out on additional profits from your book by not offering an audio version.

We have published our books in audiobook format in two different ways:

1) We have recorded the audiobook ourselves and then sold it from our website.
2) We have published audiobooks using Amazon's Audiobook Creation Exchange program or ACX.

However, when we decided to publish our audiobooks using ACX, we saw a huge increase in our overall income. This is because ACX publishes it on Audible, Amazon, and iTunes which gives it much more exposure.

The Five Steps to Publishing Your AudioBook

Step #1: Decide where to sell your audiobook.

Will you sell your audiobook on your website or through the self-publishing platform ACX? If you choose a non-exclusive contract with ACX, you can do both.

Step #2: Decide who will record your audiobook.

Most of the time you will want to hire a narrator. ACX has an option where you can hire a narrator with no upfront costs. It requires that you sign an exclusive contract and split your royalties 50/50 with your narrator, but is a great way to get started on a small budget.

You can also record your audiobook yourself if you have the right equipment. You then would need to edit your audiobook as well.

Step #3: Prepare for production.

If you decided to record the audiobook yourself, gather your equipment and everything you need to get started. We use the free audio recording and editing software, Audacity. You can download it for free here: audacity.sourceforge.net, and it is also powerful audio editing software. I (Shelley) use a higher quality microphone—the Blue Yeti USB Microphone. I also recommend that you use a pop filter for your microphone to remove sharp "B" and "P" sounds. Visit www.amazon.com/gp/product/B0002H0H4A to see the pop filter I use with my Blue Yeti USB Microphone.

If hiring a narrator, choose your narrator and submit a contract.

Step #4: Record the audiobook.

Finish recording it yourself or if hiring a narrator, approve the final audiobook files.

Step #5: Start selling your audiobook!

We highly recommend that you diversify your income by publishing your book in audiobook format. If you are interested in recording an audiobook and want more step-by-step details and resources, check out our book, "How to Publish and Market AudioBooks," here: www.trainingauthors.com/books/how-to-publish-and-market-audiobooks

CHAPTER NINE

Translating Your Book

Have you thought about translating your book and getting it published in other languages? Since I (Shelley) published my first book in 2008, I have thought about this possibility. But, it did not become a reality until this week. As of Christmas Eve, I now have one of my books published in Spanish! What a great Christmas present for me this year.

And now that I know the process, I plan to have some of our other books translated as well. But, first I wanted to share my experience with you and wanted to share how to translate your book in this tutorial.

Why Should You Translate Your Book into Other Languages?

If you have followed me very long, you know that I am all about getting the most out of the content you write. Whether it is a blog post or a book, there are many ways to repurpose your hard work.

One way to repurpose the hard work you put into writing your book is to publish it in many different formats:

- Print Book
- eBook
- AudioBook

However, you can also have your book translated into multiple languages. In my research, I did not find much information about the most popular languages to publish in on Kindle, but I did see someone say that Spanish and German seem to be on the top of the list after English. Other languages to consider are French, Italian, Japanese, Portuguese, and Chinese.

At the time of writing this post, there are 34 languages supported by KDP including:

Afrikaans

Alsatian

Basque

Bokmål Norwegian

Breton

Catalan

Cornish

Corsican

Danish

Dutch/Flemish

Eastern Frisian

English

Finnish

French

Frisian

Galician

German

Icelandic

Irish

Italian

Japanese

Luxembourgish

Manx

Northern Frisian

Norwegian

Nynorsk Norwegian

Portuguese

Provençal

Romansh

Scots

Scottish Gaelic

Spanish

Swedish

Welsh

See KDP's list of languages here:

kdp.amazon.com/help?ie=UTF8&topicId=A2AH1EAPH0YKI9

When you publish your book in other languages you will not only be able to reach more people with your message, but you will also diversify your income. There is less competition in many of these other languages which gives you the opportunity to potentially sell more books.

How I Got Started Translating My Book into Spanish

In the last five years, I have been approached several times by people who wanted to translate my books. A few people offered to translate my book *"Mirror Mirror"* for teen girls into other languages, but those opportunities always fell through. I think they meant well, but when it was on a volunteer basis, it just never got done. I also had a major Christian publisher contact me about obtaining the rights to translate my book, *"21 Prayers of Gratitude"* into Korean about a year ago. But nothing ever came of that opportunity either.

I thought that publishing my books into other languages was not possible and had given up on the idea.

That is, until I took Rachel Rofe's course, "Your Book Monopoly." In this course she shows authors how to take your book and create multiple streams of income by publishing print books, eBooks, audiobooks, getting your book into libraries and bookstores, _and_ having your book translated into other languages.

My virtual ears perked up at the last option. And I wondered…*"Could I take the information Rachel shared and publish our books in other languages?"*

I decided to start the process and find out.

How to Get Your Book Translated

In Rachel Rofe's course she shows you quotes she got for her book to be translated in Spanish and Chinese. You can hear her explain it in the video she posted on her blog that I embedded below or in the screenshot. However, she found it much cheaper to use Elance to hire a translator.

(You can learn more about Rachel's course here: www.trainingauthors.com/bookmonopoly)

My Choice: Outsourcing Through Elance

I did not have thousands of dollars in our budget to have a book translated. Therefore, I decided to try Rachel's suggestion and posted a job on Elance. I had never used Elance before and was a little nervous about the process.

I chose my best-selling book, "*21 Prayers of Gratitude*" and followed Rachel's exact outline she gives in the course. I priced my job similar to hers and posted the job online at Elance. Within hours, I had over 20 proposals of contractors willing to translate my book at a very low cost.

I then researched those who put in a proposal and looked for the following:

- They followed my directions in the job posting.
- They had a history of previous jobs on Elance.

- They had a high rating from previous jobs on Elance.

There was one person in particular that stood out to me. I contacted her and asked her if she would be willing to sign a Non-Disclosure Agreement (NDA). By signing the NDA, she would legally agree that she would only use my book contents for translation purposes only and that my publishing company, Body and Soul Publishing, would remain the sole owner of the content. The NDA was something Rachel recommended, but was not provided in her training so I came up with one on my own.

My translator agreed and we started the process. Her bid was slightly higher than some of the other contractors, but she had a longer history of completed jobs on Elance and a higher rating than most of the others (4.9/5 star rating). She was also willing to complete the small book (~5,000 words) in only 3 days.

An Important Step: Use a Proofreader/Editor

In "Your Book Monopoly," Rachel Rofe mentions the importance of using a proofreader/editor within the process. She suggests several ways to find someone that can proofread the translated book. This is an important step so that you can check the work of your contractor and make sure your content is being translated in the correct way.

I chose one of her suggested options and hired someone to proofread the translated version of my book in Spanish. I decided to pay about 45% of what I paid my translator. I did not have a reason for choosing this price, but simply chose what I thought would be fair.

Thankfully, my proofreader confirmed that it was a good translation and only had a few recommended changes. I was now ready to format my book and publish it.

Format and Publish

I then formatted my book for Kindle and CreateSpace. Once my book was published on Kindle, I posted a new project on ACX to have the Spanish version published as an audiobook as well.

I then had the book cover changed to include the Spanish title. I decided to keep everything else the same as it saved me any extra costs as I could edit the text on my cover and easily.

Here is the finished product:

21 Oraciones de Gratitud

You can find it on Kindle here: amazon.com/dp/B00HHMZ6OY

Lessons Learned

There were a few lessons I learned in the process:

#1: Have everything you need translated

- Book Description
- Your Bio
- Opt-In Page
- E-mails in Your Autoresponder

I had to go back and ask my translator to translate my book description and bio for me later. She was gracious to do it even though I had already paid her and the job was over.

I also learned that Google translate can help if you are in a bind. I would _not_ use it to translate your book, but I did use it a few times to translate text I used in my e-mail autoresponder. I did take Spanish in high school and in college, so I felt comfortable enough to know if the translation was accurate. However, next time I will have everything I need ready in advance to have translated.

#2: Use Spanish specific categories on Amazon via KDP

Each language will be different, but I found that when I chose normal categories in KDP, it listed my book as an English book on the Amazon sites for Mexico and Spain. Therefore, I researched the exact categories I wanted for those two Spanish speaking countries and requested the change manually through KDP's support.

Also, within KDP, there is a specific category for each language that you can choose. I went back and changed my categories so that it would be listed in the Spanish books. This would allow my target audience to find it easier.

- All Spanish Books:
  www.amazon.com/s/ref=nb_sb_noss?url=node%3D773
  5161011&field-keywords=&rh=n%3A133140011%2Cn%3
  A154606011%2Cn%3A7735160011%2Cn%3A7735161011
- Spanish Fiction Books:
  www.amazon.com/b/ref=dp_brlad_entry?ie=UTF8&
  node=7588769011

In order to get the book in the category: "**Kindle Store > Kindle eBooks > Foreign Languages > Spanish**", the language setting of the book needs to be "Spanish".

To change the language setting of your book, please follow the steps below:

1) Log in: kdp.amazon.com
2) Find the book you want to update, and in the "Other Book Actions" column, click "Edit book details."
3) Under the "Language" section, please change it from English to Spanish.
4) Go to the bottom of the page and click "Save and Continue."
5) Confirm that you have all rights to publish by clicking on the box at the bottom.
6) Click on "Save & Publish."

It is a learning process and I am sure I will learn a lot more along the way!

Marketing Tips

Here are a few marketing tips for you to consider once you publish your book in another language.

Start a new e-mail list specific to that language:

Create a simple opt-in page for anyone interested in knowing when I release new books in that language. I also added a link to that page in the front and back of my book.

Example: www.bodyandsoulpublishing.com/libros-espanoles-cristianos

Recruit reviewers:

Look at other Spanish books similar to yours and contact their Amazon reviewers

Check with your translator and/or proofreader to see if they know of anyone who would be interested in reviewing your book. They might be willing to ask their family and friends.

Additional Resources

1) <u>Your Book Monopoly</u> – If you would like more training on how to translate your books, I recommend Rachel Rofe's course, "Your Book Monopoly." It is the exact training I used when translating my first book. Plus you will also learn how to get your book into bookstores, libraries and more. www.trainingauthors.com/bookmonopoly

2) <u>Translation Publishing Treasures</u> – Deb & Amy also have a course, "Translation Publishing Treasures," on getting your book translated in other languages. www.trainingauthors.com/translationtreasures

Another Option

I recently found out about another option available to translate your book and publish it in other languages. It is called "Babel Cube." (www.babelcube.com) I have not personally used it yet, but they will translate and publish your book at no upfront costs.

Check out their FAQ page for authors:
www.babelcube.com/how/rights-holders

As well as their royalties' page:
www.babelcube.com/faq/revenue-share

The downfall to their current system is that they do not have a way to check the quality of the translation done. You would have to hire a proofreader or editor yourself to ensure that the translation was done well.

Overall, this reminds me of the ACX platform for audiobooks except it is used for translating books into other languages. If you use their system, leave me a comment on your experience so we can learn from each other at:

www.trainingauthors.com/how-to-translate-your-book

PART THREE

Other Publishing Decisions

CHAPTER TEN

Obtaining a Copyright

Obtaining a copyright is about registering your work, for example, your self-published book, at a copyright office. Technically, your work is under your copyright as soon as you imprint it on a fixed device. For example, if you write a song on a piece of paper, you already have the rights to that work.

Personally, we have not officially registered our books with the copyright office. Technically our products are copyrighted as soon as we publish them. However, some authors will want this additional layer of security to ensure their work is protected. Therefore, you may want to know more about how to get a copyright and determine if it is the best option for you.

The Top 8 Most Important Tips on How to Get a Copyright:

#1: Obtaining a Copyright is Easy.

The first step is to research the laws for the country in which you live.

To have your book copyrighted in the U.S., you simply need to register your work in a copyright office. If it is possible, they will keep a copy of your work. Whenever someone else claims they are the owner, the copyright office will compare their work with the copy you left at their office. As a result, they will reject the claim of the other person.

#2: Obtaining a Copyright is Relatively Inexpensive.

If your work is going to bring you money, you should consider registering the work and pay a fee. The registration fees range between a few dozen and a few hundred dollars.

#3: You Need to be the First Author.

How to get a copyright involves being the first author of the work. It does not matter if you are the second person who created the exact same work. Only the first one counts.

#4: Copyrighting can be Hard to Prove.

How can you prove that you are the first owner of a work? Unless you register the work it is hard to prove. Of course, there are ways to do it. As a singer, you can sign the song during a concert and be filmed. And as an author, you can print a copy of your book and mail it to yourself. You then keep the envelope unopened to have a date on it if you ever need to prove the work is yours.

#5: Your Boss will Hold the Copyright if You are the One Hired for the Job.

A person hired (e.g., ghostwriter) will not own the copyright of that work. The person paying the ghostwriter not only buys the work but also becomes the owner of the copyright as well.

#6: Your Work is Protected from Derivative Works as Well.

According to the copyright definition, derivative works use one or more parts of the copyrighted work. A rewritten article is a derivative work.

In the US, there is also the "fair use". You can find out more about fair use here: www.copyright.gov/fls/fl102.html

#7: You Receive the Copyright by Default.

As soon as you create a work, you are the rightful copyright owner of that work. You don't have to think about how to get a copyright. You received it by doing nothing. The problem is that you are the only person who knows about it.

#8: How to Protect Yourself in Court.

Let's say that you create a work but you did not register it at the U.S. copyrighting office. If someone uses your work as their own, you cannot win a lawsuit against them by default. You need to prove that you were the first person who created the work. That is pretty much impossible to do. This is why it is important to consider whether or not you want to register the work right from the beginning.

If the copyright registration of your book is done within five years from its creation, it is considered "prima facie" evidence in court. This means that if you ever went to court, the registration of your copyright would be enough evidence of your ownership of the copyrighted material.

Every author's situation is different. Therefore, it is important to decide whether or not you want to take this extra step of registering a copyright for your book.

CHAPTER ELEVEN

How to Form an Independent Publishing Company

Disclaimer: *The content in this chapter is for informational purposes only. I am not a lawyer or accountant and am not giving legal advice. Consult with a tax professional and lawyer before making decisions regarding your business.*

As an author, have you considered starting your own independent publishing company? Many self-published authors are now choosing this option. In fact, this is what my husband CJ and I have done. We started Body and Soul Publishing in 2012 and have not looked back yet.

Three Reasons to Start an Independent Publishing Company

#1: It Looks More Professional.

When you start an independent publishing company, you can then register your ISBN with your company name as the publisher. This will show up on your book sales page and looks more professional than "CreateSpace" or "your name" as the publisher.

#2: It Separates Your Book Publishing Activities from your Personal Income and Assets.

It can be helpful to have your business and personal finances separate for tax purposes. In fact, sometimes it can save you money!

Also, when you form a LLC or S-corp, it shields your personal income and assets from lawsuits that may occur. Lawsuits are very rare in our type of business, but some people prefer to have this extra layer of protection in place.

#3: It Gives You More Options.

Once you establish your independent publishing company, you have more options. You may even choose to publish other author's books with your publishing company listed as the publisher.

10 Steps to Forming an Independent Publishing Company

#1: Make a Decision

The first step to starting your own publishing company is to make the decision. You need to decide that you want to make writing and publishing books a business and not just a hobby.

This is a huge mindset shift for most authors.

And a necessary one. I found that once I made this decision in 2012, I became much more serious about investing into my publishing business. And as I focused more on book marketing, my career as an author took off.

Are you ready? If so, it's time to go to step #2.

#2: Research Your Options

Now it is time to research your options. Make sure to know what options are available in your country. Since I live in the US, I researched three main options:

- Sole Proprietorship
- LLC
- S-Corporation

A sole proprietorship is an unincorporated business that you run yourself. In the US, you claim this under your social security number for taxes. This is the easiest way to start. As a sole proprietor it will still technically be under your SSN but you can get a federal EIN to use. This is what we did and filed a DBA "doing business as" using our publishing company name. This is filed at the state level. Here is some more info: www.sba.gov/content/register-your-fictitious-or-doing-business-dba-name

An LLC is a limited liability company that is taxed similarly to a sole proprietorship. However it is an incorporated business and separates and protects your personal assets from business assets under limited liability.

An S-Corporation is an incorporated business and gives more tax advantages and savings.

Although you don't need to know every detail about each option, I do think it is wise to do some basic research before consulting with experts.

#3: Consult With Experts

It is important to consult with experts before making decisions about your business. Many lawyers and accountants offer a free consultation to answer your questions. They can advise you on the best path for your particular situation.

For my husband and me, it was recommended that we start an LLC that is taxed as an S-Corp as this would save us thousands of dollars in self-employment taxes. However, each person's situation is different. So, make sure to consult with a lawyer and an accountant for advice on how to proceed.

#4: Decide on a Business Name

Once you decide on which type of business to set up, you now have the responsibility of choosing a name. Ensure your name is not trademarked or already taken in your state if you live in the US.

You also want to choose a business name that is professional and fits your brand. Don't rush this step as your business name will stay with you a long time!

#5: Finalize the Business Type

Now that you have your business name chosen, you can finalize the set-up of your publishing company. When we first started Body and Soul Publishing as a sole proprietorship, I filed a DBA (doing business as) with my state. I then received paperwork that listed my EIN (employer identification number) which would allow me to open a business bank account. I also used that EIN to file 1099's for my contractors and to file my taxes for our business.

However, once we decided to incorporate as an LLC, we had our tax guy set it up for us. He charged a minimal fee and made sure it was done correctly.

#6: Set Up Your Business Bank Account

Once you have your EIN, you can now apply for a business bank account. Each bank has a different process and requirements for setting up a business account. Therefore, consult with your local bank for more details.

You may also want to set up a business PayPal account for transactions online.

#7: Set Up an Accounting System

Bookkeeping used to be a bad word in our house. However, once we learned how to properly use accounting software and set up our bookkeeping correctly, it actually helped to decrease our stress.

We consulted with an accounting service and paid a small fee to have them help us set everything up. She recommended that we buy the cheapest version of Quick Books we could find at an office supplies store. She said she preferred the computer software versus the online version as it gives you more control, it is easier to export data for your accountant or bookkeeper, and it tends to be cheaper.

Make sure you implement a system for tracking your receipts. You also want to be very careful to never buy personal items with a business account and vice versa. You want to be organized and keep things separate. This will make life much easier come tax time!

#8: Register a Domain Name for Your Business

I highly recommend you register a domain name for your business. This is another way to add more professionalism to your company. It can also be a place where you post a listing of your published books. I have started using the My Book Table plugin (www.authormedia.com/mybooktable) on my author site and recommend it. It makes it super easy to add book pages and buy links for your books. You can see how I set it up here: shelleyhitz.com/bookshelf.

#9: Learn the Laws Related to Your Business

Make sure you learn the laws related to your business. For example, in the US, there are laws about collecting sales tax when you sell books at live events and it differs from state to state. You may also need to register for a sales tax license in your state and/or your city.

#10: Celebrate Your Success!

Now it is time to celebrate your success. You have formed your own independent publishing company!

My Personal Story

In 2012, we started our independent publishing company. Initially, we created a sole proprietorship because it was the easiest way to start with the least expense.

However, in 2014, my husband and I got hit really hard by taxes. Therefore, we decided to set up an appointment with a local "tax guy." Fortunately, our appointment went really well and we decided to officially incorporate our business as an LLC, filing taxes as an S-Corp. We have a long to-do list, but I am confident that next year will not be as stressful, which is such a relief!

The bad news? If we would have consulted with this same "tax guy" last year, he could have saved us thousands of dollars on self-employment taxes this year.

Ouch.

We will definitely be hiring him to do our taxes next year! Even though this is the case for us, please note that every author's situation is unique. That is why it is important to consult with expert advice prior to making any big decisions. We found our tax guy through Dave Ramsey's endorsed local providers list (www.daveramsey.com/elp/tax-services).

Have you ever learned a lesson the hard way?

I have many times.

And it seems I learn more from my mistakes than I do from my successes. It is in the difficult and painful seasons of life that I grow the most.

I'll be honest...there are days I feel like giving up. I ask myself, "Is this really worth it?"

Occasionally God will give me a small glimpse of the impact my life is having on others. In fact, this very week I was encouraged by two authors that personally thanked me for helping them publish and market their books. They are both successful authors today.

So I will close with some encouragement for you (and for myself) as we embark on this journey of writing and publishing books.

"Never, never, never give up!"

I encourage you to learn from your mistakes and keep making progress toward your publishing goals one step at a time.

Self-Publishing in a Nutshell

We have So there you have the basics to self-publishing a book. We have covered the cost of self-publishing, book layout/design, different self-publishing companies, software option, and so much more. In a world that is constantly changing, we encourage you to stay up to date with the self-publishing industry. One of the ways to do that is to sign up for our free newsletter at: www.trainingauthors.com/newsletter

You can also find more information about self-publishing on our website: www.trainingauthors.com

Before we close this book, I (Shelley) wanted to include the step-by-step process to self-publishing a book from start to finish. After all, knowing is only half the battle. Obviously you have to start by writing the book, and will end with the marketing, but here's a quick run through of everything that comes in between:

Step One: Foundation for Publishing Success

- Write Your Book
- Edit Your Book
- Start Building Your Marketing Platform (e.g., blog, website, Facebook, Twitter, YouTube, etc.)

Step Two: Self-Publishing Your Book

- Make Pre-Publication Decisions (book title, book description, pricing, categories/keywords, etc.)
- Have Your Book Cover Designed
- Self-Publish a Print Book
- Self-Publish an eBook
- Self-Publish an AudioBook
- Translate Your Book

Step Three: Other Publishing Decisions

- Obtain a Copyright
- Form an Independent Publishing Company

You should now be well equipped to self-publish your book. We wish you the best on your journey!

Next Steps

As soon as your book is published, we encourage you to set up these 2 important author profiles.

1) Sign up for Amazon Author Central - This is a must for every published author. It is your author profile on Amazon and allows you to preform edits to your book description, see sales data, and more—all in one place. You can learn more about using Amazon as an author in Marketing Your Book on Amazon—we have include an excerpt from that book in the appendix.

2) Become a Goodreads Author – Goodreads is one of the most visited reader sites around and they have great marketing options for authors (some of them free). If you would like to learn more about it, Rachelle Gardner wrote a great piece on "How Authors Can Effectively Use Goodreads" over at Books & Such (www.booksandsuch.com/blog/how-authors-can-effectively-use-goodreads). We do highly recommend adding your book to their database and setting up that profile as soon as you have a chance.

Each of those profiles will help you on your journey to reaching success as an author. But they are just two steps on your journey. And that's what marketing your book is—a journey.

Many people have related the process of being an author to that of being a parent. Writing your book is like the pregnancy part. Developing your book is part of who you are and is constantly there. You are always thinking about how great it will be, but it is just the beginning. Towards the end your anticipation and anxiety grow. And then you finally reach the publishing process—which is like the delivery. But then you are left with a lifetime of book rearing. The real journey doesn't end at publication, it begins.

As an author and a mom, one thing I (Heather) want to leave you with is a quote from Jane D. Hull, "At the end of the day, the most overwhelming key to a child's success is the positive involvement of parents." The same is true for our books. Their success depends on positive involvement from the authors. The more you believe in your book and its value, the more you work at getting it noticed, the more likely it will be to succeed.

In part one, we covered building a book marketing platform to get you set up for success (that's like preparing the nursery before a baby is born), but here are a few additional tips to get you started being an involved and successful author:

#1: Solicit Book Reviews

Getting honest reviews of your book is one of the best ways to let others know how awesome it is. We have 7 methods we use to get reviews for our books. They are:

- Ask Your Sphere of Influence

- Contact Amazon Reviewers
- Harness the Power of Social Media Groups
- Contact Blog Reviewers
- Conduct Giveaways to Get Reviews
- Develop a Book Review Program

In our book, *"How to Get Honest Reviews"* we go into much more details, teach authors how to contact reviewers, and so much more. You can find out more here: www.trainingauthors.com/books/honest-reviews

#2: Have a Book Launch

Book launches are a great way to get the word out about your new book. We recommend having some reviews for your book prior to your launch, which is why this is second.

#3: Learn all You Can About Book Marketing

There are infinite ways to market your books. You might check out our book, "Author Publicity Pack" to get ideas on where you can advertise. Or read my book, "A Year of Book Marketing" to stay encouraged and generate ideas.

You'll find even more book marketing resources listed in the appendix to help you on your journey. You can check out our blog for helpful articles on writing, publishing, and marketing your books. And you might want to pick up the second book in this series, "Book Marketing 101."

No matter where you go from here, know that we are cheering you on!

To your success,
Shelley Hitz and Heather Hart

TrainingAuthors.com

P.S. As you know (or will soon find out), reviews are gold to authors.

If you have found this book helpful, would you consider leaving an honest review on Amazon?

Marketing Your Book On Amazon

21 THINGS YOU CAN EASILY DO FOR FREE TO GET MORE EXPOSURE AND SALES

by Shelley Hitz

Once you publish your book on Amazon, it's time to start marketing it. Unfortunately, very few books become bestsellers overnight. Instead, many authors become discouraged at the lack of sales and results. I encourage authors to see book marketing as a marathon, not a sprint. Book marketing expert, John Kremer says, "Do something every day to market each of your books for three years."

However, there are many things you can easily do for free after publication to market your book on Amazon for both print and Kindle eBooks. I published my first book in November of 2008. I wish that I would have known the strategies that I am going to teach you in this book four years ago as it would have resulted in more exposure and potentially many more sales. Better late than never!

Over and over I have seen authors neglect to take the steps I have outlined in this book. I believe that what I share provides a strong foundation for the rest of your marketing efforts. If you fail to implement these simple, but effective strategies, your overall marketing plan will not be as effective. So take the time to go through each of these steps for each of your books.

Powerful Results By Optimizing Book Categories

One of the most powerful things I am going to teach you within these pages is how to choose the best category for your book. It is amazing what a few tweaks and changes to your Amazon account can do for your book rankings! Within just a few days of optimizing one of my books, it hit #1 on Kindle for its category.

Amazon Best Sellers Rank: #27,046 Paid in Kindle Store

#1 in Kindle Store > Kindle eBooks > Nonfiction > Children's Nonfiction > Religions > Christianity > Prayer

And I have seen similar results over and over with my other books.

Are You Selling As Many Books As You Would Like?

If not, it might be because people are not finding you. One way to increase your exposure on Amazon's search engine is through keywords. Have you chosen the most effective keywords for your book? I will also cover how to research and update the keywords for your book, both for print books and Kindle eBooks.

I truly believe that optimizing your book sales page on Amazon is one of the most effective things you can do to market your book(s). Want to know the crazy part about this? It's free! All it will cost you is a few hours of your time.

So What Are You Waiting For?

Let's get started!

Watch a free 43 minute video tutorial from Shelley and get your copy of this book here: www.trainingauthors.com/books/marketing-your-book-on-amazon

ADDITIONAL RESOURCES

Book Marketing Survival Guide Tool Kit

Access our database of templates, trainings and more with our Survival Guide Tool Kit. Find out more here:
www.trainingauthors.com/toolkit

Our Books for Authors

We have an entire library of books for authors, including books on publishing and marketing. Check out the entire list here:
www.trainingauthors.com/books

Recommended Outsourcers for Authors

If you need help with the technical side of publishing and marketing your books, consider outsourcing to one of our recommended providers here:
www.trainingauthors.com/recommended-outsourcers for-authors

Tools and Resources We Use and Recommend

Check out the tools we use and recommend for writing, publishing and marketing here:
www.trainingauthors.com/resources

THE BOOK MARKETING SURVIVAL GUIDE SERIES

Are you fighting to survive the journey of marketing your book?

If so, we invite you to gear up with the Book Marketing Survival Guide Series.

Ranging in topics from how to run a book launch, to networking, to offline marketing, this series has something for every author—no matter what stage of the book marketing journey you are in. Each survival guide has a matching toolkit available where authors can access templates, checklists, video tutorials and more on the topic covered in the book.

Find out more at:

www.trainingauthors.com/books/#SurvivalGuides

ABOUT THE AUTHORS

Shelley Hitz and Heather Hart work as a team to help authors succeed. They have been working together since 2009 and have been referred to as the "writer's dynamic duo". One of the ways they help authors is by sharing their about their own experiences in the book industry.

Shelley Hitz

Shelley Hitz is an award-winning and internationally best-selling author. She is the owner of TrainingAuthors.com and is passionate about helping authors succeed in publishing and marketing their books.

And she teaches from personal experience. Shelley has been writing and publishing books since 2008 and has published over 30 books including print, eBook and audio book formats.

Heather Hart

Heather Hart is a book marketing expert, internationally best-selling author, and is the manager of TrainingAuthors.com. With the heart of an author, Heather enjoys working from home where she spends her days typing away at her computer, brainstorming new marketing ideas, and encouraging those around her.

Her desire is to help others successfully publish and market their books while continuing to author, contribute to, and market multiple book marketing and faith-based books herself – and have fun doing it.

Access Their FREE Author Training Here:
www.TrainingAuthors.com/Newsletter

See A Complete List Of Their Books For Authors Here:
www.TrainingAuthors.com/Books

Connect with Shelley and Heather Online

www.facebook.com/trainingauthors

www.twitter.com/trainingauthors

www.youtube.com/trainingauthors

CPSIA information can be obtained at www.ICGtesting.com
Printed in the USA
LVOW07s1542160315

430764LV00024B/2393/P